The Way of
Nile C. Kinnick, Jr.

The Way of
Nile C. Kinnick, Jr.

Insights, Images, and
Stories of Iowa's 1939
Heisman Trophy Winner

Mark D. Wilson

Mark D. Wilson

INDIANA
vs. IOWA
DAD'S DAY
OCTOBER 7, 1939

Ice Cube Press, LLC
North Liberty, Iowa, USA

The Way of Nile C. Kinnick, Jr.: Insights, Images, and Stories of Iowa's 1939 Heisman Trophy Winner

Copyright © 2018 Mark D. Wilson
Epilogue © 2018 James A. Leach

First Edition

ISBN 9781948509015

Library of Congress Control Number: 2018939529

Ice Cube Press, LLC (Est. 1991) | North Liberty, Iowa 52317
www.icecubepress.com | steve@icecubepress.com

The paper used in this publication meets the minimum requirements of the American National Standard for Information Sciences— Permanence of Paper for Printed Library Materials, ANSI Z39.48-1992.

Manufactured in Canada

Thanks to David McCartney at The University of Iowa Libraries Special Collections for assistance in this project.

Photos and images on pages 15-21, 51, 52, 54, 55, 57, 59, 60, 62-69, 102, 103, 106, 107, 135, 138, 144 are used with permission of Papers of Nile Kinnick (collection MsC 112), Department of Special Collections and University Archives, The University of Iowa Libraries.

Additionally: photos and images on pages 53, 56, 58, 61, 70, 104, 139-143, 145-150 including football program covers are used with Permission of Mark Wilson's Hawkeye Collection. Photos and images on pages 136, 137 used with Permission Jim Heims' Hawkeye Collection. Photos and images pages 151-154 used with Permission of Lonny Tanner's Hawkeye Collection. Bottom photo page 151 from https://en.wikipedia.org/wiki/Nile_C._Kinnick_High_School. Photo on page 105 used with Permission of David Dierks' Hawkeye Collection.

Appreciation

This book is dedicated to all Iowa Hawkeye fans who are fascinated with the legendary Nile Clarke Kinnick, Jr., a man respected for his remarkable athleticism and leadership on the football field, his academic achievements, and his service to his country.

After Nile's death on June 2, 1943, during WW II, the late Dr. Virgil Hancher, former president of The State University of Iowa, wrote a letter to Kinnick's parents, Nile, Sr. and Frances:

> "... I do wish to pay tribute to the qualities which made him not only an outstanding athlete but a remarkable student and gentlemen as well. It would have been very easy for a young man of his years to be affected by the great praise which was heaped upon him, but never by word or act was there a false note in his conduct.
>
> "His life until June 2 was as near perfection as anything I expect to see in my time here. The inspiration of his example has affected and will continue to affect his college generation. The tragedy of his death is that the qualities and abilities which he possessed will be so much needed in the years after the war..."

The royalties of this book are being donated to The University of Iowa Center for Advancement to help fund six scholarships named after Nile Clarke Kinnick, Jr. They are: the Nile Kinnick Leadership Scholarship, four Nile Kinnick Memorial Scholarships, and the Nile Kinnick Scholarship for Women.

Hopefully, readers will glean personal meaning from the insights of Nile, a man, "...typifying everything admirable in American youth." (Whitney Martin, AP Writer, *Des Moines Register*, December 8, 1939.)

Contents

Preface

∽

Nile Clarke Kinnick, Jr. was an outstanding student-athlete at The State University of Iowa, a role model, a leader, and an inspiration to many. He was president of his class, a Phi Beta Kappa scholar, and won numerous awards in football including the Heisman, Walter Camp, and Maxwell trophies for being the best college football player in the United States of America.

The late Tait Cummins, a Cedar Rapids, Iowa, WMT television and radio sportscaster, once said of Nile: "Everything that can be said that is good about college athletes he was; he didn't represent it…he was it."

During World War II, Nile lost his life while serving his country on a training mission as a pilot in the US Naval Air Corps Reserve. Excerpts from his diaries, journals, letters, and speeches in this compilation are not only inspirational, but reflect Kinnick's moral character, mature idealism, humor, humility, compassion, and leadership. His articulate oratory and writing style are both descriptive and enlightening. His sentiments, convictions, and wisdom about war, economics, social issues, education, government, politics, and numerous other topics are still relevant and useful today.

The Man in the Arena

On April 23, 1910, Theodore Roosevelt, the 26th President of the United States, gave a thirty-five page speech at the University of Paris. Roosevelt's speech entitled, *Citizenship in a Republic*, emphasized that the success of its people relied upon disciplined work and character. The former President told the assembled audience that "self-restraint, self-mastery, common sense, the power of accepting individual responsibility, and yet of acting in conjunction with others, courage and resolution—these are the qualities which mark a masterful people."

I've included a small but significant portion of Roosevelt's speech for you to enjoy. The discourse epitomizes Nile C. Kinnick, Jr. and truly personifies Nile's grit, determination, and perseverance:

> *"It is not the critic who counts; not the man who points out how the strong man stumbles, or where the doer of deeds could have done them better. The credit belongs to the man who is actually in the arena, whose face is marred by dust and sweat and blood; who strives valiantly; who errs, who comes short again and again, because there is no effort without error and shortcoming; but who does actually strive to do the deeds; who knows great enthusiasms, the great devotions; who spends himself in a worthy cause; who at the best knows in the end the triumph of high achievement, and who at the worst, if he fails, at least fails while daring greatly, so that his place shall never be with those cold and timid souls who know neither victory nor defeat."*

—President Theodore Roosevelt

1939 Football Programs

A note on the five football programs included inside this book.

In the fall of 1939, The State University Iowa football team was about to play one of the most difficult schedules in the Nation, and unfortunately, they were predicted by pollsters to place last in the Big Ten Conference. To make things worse, except for 1933, Iowa finished the 1930s decade as one the worst three teams in the conference based on standings at season's end. That turned completely around when Dr. Edward Anderson came on board to be the next head coach for Iowa. In addition Nile Kinnick was healthy again after playing through an injury-filled season in 1938.

The five programs featured in this book are some of the greatest games played at Iowa Stadium (now Kinnick Stadium). In the first Big Ten game against Indiana (title page), Iowa trailed 29-26. With a fourth down situation, Kinnick threw a perfect pass to Irv Prasse and Iowa beat the Hoosiers 32-29.

In the Wisconsin game (pg. 1) at Madison, Iowa was down 13-12 in the fourth quarter. Kinnick threw his third touchdown pass of the day to Bill Green and Iowa held on to win 19-13.

Iowa's fifth game of the season was a Homecoming game at Ross-Ade Stadium in West Lafayette, Indiana. Purdue (pg. 32) was an early favorite to win the Conference Championship, and Iowa was once again an underdog for the third consecutive game. In the fourth quarter the Boilermakers bobbled a snap on a punt and Iowa's Mike Enich blocked the attempt. Iowa recovered the ball in the end zone for a safety. When Iowa couldn't move the ball, Kinnick had to punt. The Hawks held Purdue and they were forced to punt again. The punt was blocked by "Iron Mike" once again; Iowa pounced on the ball for a second safety, and the Hawks won 4-0.

Iowa next returned home to Iowa City to play third ranked Notre Dame (pg. 82). Iowa took the lead in the third quarter when Kinnick scored a touchdown. Nile then drop-kicked the ball for the extra point and Iowa led 7-0. The mighty Irish tried to make a comeback in the fourth quarter, but fell short when the point after touchdown was missed. Iowa went on to win one of the most historic games in Hawkeye football history, 7-6.

The fifth program featured was Iowa's Homecoming in Iowa City against another Big Ten favorite, Minnesota (pg. 119). Kinnick threw for two touchdowns and kicked an extra point. Bill Green caught the winning touchdown from Nile and the Black and Gold shocked the Gophers, 13-9. Upset after upset occurred throughout this fascinating season. What made the season even more remarkable was Iowa had thirty-five players on the roster and yet only fifteen of them played in many of the games! Dr. Eddie's players were true Ironmen.

Fascination

Chapter One

To me, Nile Clarke Kinnick, Jr. was more than just a familiar name, a distinguished scholar, and a well-known athlete. He was a fascinating young man who accomplished so much in such a short time. Nile excelled as an undergraduate and graduate student at The State University of Iowa and as a team member who played football for the Hawkeyes. Kinnick even worked part-time and was president of his senior class. After graduation, he went on to law school and volunteered to serve his country during World War II.

Nile, at the age of twenty-four, unexpectedly gave the ultimate sacrifice while on a training mission as a US Naval Air Corps

Reserve fighter pilot. On June 2, 1943, Kinnick's Grumman F4F Wildcat plane had mechanical failure due to an oil leak. As a result, he could not land his plane on the USS Lexington aircraft carrier and had to make an emergency landing in the Gulf of Paria off the coast of Venezuela. Kinnick lost his life in that crash and his body and plane were never recovered. After hearing of Kinnick's death, the late Bill Green, Sr., a 1942 graduate of The State University of Iowa, friend, teammate of Kinnick, and a trainer of fighter pilots, said of Nile:

> *"He provided dynamic leadership to our team in a humble way. How easy and at ease he kept us—he exuded hope and confidence. He was a meaningful symbol to all of Iowa. He represented all that you wanted to be. Nile was willing to work for perfection. He didn't have super talent to begin with. He was intelligent and he trained to excel."*

Green, and others who knew him well, said Nile was a tremendous athlete, a man of conviction and insight, a prolific writer, and a great public speaker. Others said he was a leader who had a future in politics and was a positive role model as well as a true gentleman.

In 2008, after years of reading and listening to stories about Kinnick, I began my dream to accumulate information from various sources to start researching this extraordinary man. I read, tagged, underlined, and wrote down facts from the material I assembled. Some of my documentation included background about his heritage, his childhood years, and his high school days in Iowa and Nebraska.

From my research, what really began to stand out were passages from Nile's astounding writing and speaking quotes. I was intrigued by his intellectual capabilities. Kinnick used his gifts to express his personal thoughts about life in general and his viewpoints on the topics of his day, such as war, politics, government, and economics. In his diaries from 1936-1943, he cited facts and editorialized his opinions about college, social issues, poverty, military training, and dozens of other topics. To Nile, these issues commanded responses, and respond he did. He shared his opinions in letters to family and friends and collected his thoughts in personal journals.

After documenting hundreds of quotes by Kinnick, I began the process of writing the book, *The Way of Nile C. Kinnick, Jr.* The book is a compilation of 366 quotes of inspiration, clever wit, and impactful wisdom. Kinnick's personal quotes show sensitive insight, and portions of his written speeches are spirited and eloquently written in a personal and professional style. Amazingly, dozens of his quotes are still closely connected to and reflective of many of today's issues, debates, and controversies. I feel that many of them continue to be significant, decades after he had written them.

Included within this book of memorable quotes, I interspersed four personal stories of my own. Nile had a tremendous influence on me, and these stories reflect my perceptions of and connections to him during his student-athlete and military service years. My fascination with Nile gave me the inspiration and labor of love to write this book over a period of ten years. Enjoy this journey into the mind of Nile Kinnick.

The Way of Nile

The First Quarter,

Part One

∽

January 1

(New Year's Day) The year 1942 will be a critical period for the democracies. Wishful thinking, unfounded optimism won't meet the test. Individually and collectively we must face the future with grim determination and courageous staying power born of a confident faith in God and in the destiny of freedom loving nations. Ours must be a daily resolve to fight through to complete victory whatever the sacrifice.

January 2

Why not "take it easy" and attempt to "be" for a while… enough time must be set aside, it seems to me, for a little contemplative thought and speculation, a little thoughtful inquiry as to whither art we bound and are we on the right track.

January 3

How are we to develop a sense of appreciation, of human understanding, of rationality, of true, harmonious living if we don't slow up and philosophize now and then.

January 4

Consideration and helpfulness are great virtues and well worth cultivating.

January 5

The happy, peaceful, kindly mind is the one which loses all sense of self and takes no thought of the physical body.

January 6

To be a tough, rugged boy is every lad's ambition. But to be a gentleman, to be kindly, charitable, thoughtful as well as tough and rugged is much more to be desired. And he who can be both is much better the man and usually much tougher in the long run. He is admired and respected by all but those who are too 'small' to acclaim fine characteristics.

January 7

Keep it up; never cease to strive for the best.

January 8

Be at ease, joyful, composed in all your activities and associations.

January 9

Do not quibble and quarrel over trivialities, but stand firm as the rock of Gibraltar on matters of principle.

January 10

(A portion of Nile's first political speech at a Young Republican meeting.) Wake up. When the members of any nation have come to regard their country as nothing more than the plot of ground on which they reside, and their government as a mere organization for providing police or contracting entities; when they have ceased to entertain any warmer feelings for one another than those which interest or personal friendship, or a mere general philanthropy may produce, the moral dissolution of that nation is at hand.

January 11

(Portion of a letter written to his brother George) Do not argue vociferously over a referee's decision or a difference in size of dessert, but stand solid and unflinching when it is a question of absolute honesty, truthfulness, kindness, compassion, thoughtfulness, etc.

January 12

Have you learned to compete? To work hard and keep going even when it isn't easy?

January 13

Truth and Love ARE efficacious; reliance thereon is PRACTICAL.

January 14

The belief that such harmony and unity of effort is impossible should not be accepted.

January 15

We should battle with a joyous feeling of confidence and absolute lack of apprehension.

January 16

Religions, convictions, philosophies may differ—widely and bitterly; but never, in my belief, should such differences be allowed to assume the personal aspect. Disassociation from people for such reasons is inexcusable; it is representative of bigotry and intolerance.

January 17

Necessity and other circumstance often alter convictions.

January 18

That "Ye shall know them by their fruits" (Matthew 7:16) is not an empty and obsolete phrase. It is only just and right thinking shall be provocative of just rewards.

January 19

The law of "Divine Principle is as powerful in the material world as in the spiritual." Victory shall be undeniably ours.

January 20

It is my belief that the essential thing to be gained from a college education is to learn to think, to think for yourself; to develop an active, alert, inquiring mind.

January 21

It would seem quite natural that we should turn to the writings of the great minds of the centuries gone by to discipline and guide our own mode of thinking.

January 22

Anytime that they or any other employer of mine or my associates disapprove or become intolerant of the principles which give birth and foster those characteristics which they originally professed to admire—they making no correlation, or appreciation of the cause and effect between principle and external characteristic—we then have met the parting of the ways.

January 23

The world is alive, alert, and dynamic. So must we be. It is an opportunity, not a problem.

January 24

Don't read and parrot back in the language of another; don't think and explain through the already formed concepts of someone else all the time.

January 25

Don't be afraid to grasp, develop and expound your own ideas. "An expert is often just a glib fellow away from home."

January 26

I am interested in government and have some ambition in that direction. Politics are not very clean but they should be; politics need integrity and idealism; politics more often than not disillusion those who enter with those ideas. Of that I am fully aware. But that does not alter the situation…I shall proceed as best I can—and whether I lose 50% popular favor shall not deter me…I am doing what I think is the right thing to do.

January 27

It seems to me absolutely necessary, and in reality a joy, that a young man starting out in the world should be imbued with a desire to benefit mankind and society by his work and service—whether that be in the field business, law, or something else.

January 28

(About mathematics and calculus) The important thing, it seems to me, is to study both of these fields enough to start you on the right track—the processes of scientific logic, etc., and then eagerly to turn to the current problems facing your locality, your state, nation and world today.

January 29

Mathematics also provides a fertile field for mental gymnastics and development of logic. But that there is a close correlation between intensive study of calculus and clear and concise reasoning on practical problems in later life, I seriously doubt.

January 30

Study history and economics in order that you may see the possible why and wherefore of the current events of the day.

January 31

Man should be motivated in searching for employment and finding his place in society by the desire to benefit his fellow man and society, to leave his community and country a better place in which to live insofar as his effort, humble as it may be, will help produce that result.

February 1

(Nile wrote this the day before he reported for active duty, just three days prior to the Japanese attack on Pearl Harbor) May God give me the courage and ability to so conduct myself in every situation that my country, my family and my friends will be proud of me.

February 2

(About World War II) How ridiculously short-sighted this sudden war has made the isolationists look…Oh, that this country and England had had the courage to forestall all this when Japan first went into Manchukua and Italy into Abyssinia. Sacrificing principle to temporary expediency is always costly in the long run. There is no correct road except straight ahead.

February 3

Study literature in order that you may improve your mode of expression; in order that you may more clearly and conclusively express your ideas and convictions on the problem of the day.

February 4

The great men in literature and philosophy claim our problems to be entirely philosophic and religious, and proceed to analyze everything on a philosophic basis but can't offer a thing on the practical, positive side.

February 5

The economists and sociologists weakly admit that our entire problem is lack of a "good neighbor" policy, a "love your neighbors as yourself" philosophy, then proceed energetically to label everything as a social and economic problem and attempt just as energetically to solve it on that basis.

February 6

In reality you have to educate yourself. College only presents the opportunity. Only you, yourself, know the best way for you to get what you want and to what degree you are getting it.

February 7

Decide what should be gotten from each course, ie., what you desire to get, and study it with that goal in mind and not the ultimate grade.

February 8

Too much time is spent getting ready to live and making a living and not enough in living dynamically and right now.

February 9

More time should be spent trying to understand the problems of universal import—economical, physical, social, etc.—in order that we may live better and more fully and interestedly; in order that we may be better prepared to aid humanity and the world.

February 10

I am very much in favor of studying history and economics in the light of present day conditions, in comparing and evaluating a similar period of the past with the future, in absorbing the fundamental principles of economics and analyzing the present economic problems in that light.

February 11

The most important thing—and I am sure I am right—is to maintain an active, alert interest in everything around you.

February 12

Analyze and think for yourself. Read and listen only insofar as it stimulates and aids your own thinking.

February 13

We need a coalition government…as well as the services of the best men in the country regardless of party…Whether Roosevelt is a big enough man to do this I don't know. He seems to have unconquerable aversion toward those who have opposed him.

February 14

St. Valentines Day—patron saint of lovers —which still leaves me outside the fold—how sad.

February 15

Develop an active, dynamic interest. Read, discuss and understand; think for yourself and gradually form your opinions and convictions (about them).

February 16

The only thing that bothers me about going into business is could I do people more good somewhere else? I think that is the main point naive as it may seem.

February 17

Is it logic or organizations which rule an organized society?

February 18

Be alert, inquire, question, read, discuss, understand.

February 19

(Nile's hyperbole) This morning was absolutely perfect for flying. The air was smooth as silk, the sun shone brightly, everything was just right. No one who has not flown on such a day can appreciate the feeling of exultant joy it gives… Officially assumed my duties as Right Wing Commander.

February 20

It is remarkable what a refreshing tonic a pretty girl can be.

February 21

What is man's obligation to society—I know your answer, but does it run farther than that practically?

February 22

I am more and more becoming set against obscuring initiative, imagination and ideas by too much detail, mediocre conservatism and directed study. All this is not a camouflage for laziness or an apology for possible low grades in the future. It is at present my firm conviction. I trust I have the courage to practice it.

February 23

(About military training) The physical education instructors have given strength tests to all students the past few days…my effort…8 feet and two inches standing broad jump, 31 back levers, 16 chin-ups, 40 push ups for a total of 354 points—80 points higher than anyone else—the instructors seem to think it is a pretty good mark to shoot at.

Photographs
Childhood

Nile Clarke Kinnick, Jr. at nine months.

Nile, Sr. with Nile (left) and Ben getting ready to play catch.

Nile and his younger brother Ben getting ready for a little football practice. (1920s)

Ben hiking the football to Nile outside their home in Adel, Iowa.

Six-year-old Nile posing with his football. (1924)

Nile on his paper route delivering the *Des Moines Register.* (1928)

Frances Kinnick watches sons, Nile and Ben, play the game "Four in a Row" while brother George looks on.

Nile Clark Kinnick, Sr. with sons George, Nile, and Ben.

Nile with his dad and mom on high school graduation day in Omaha, Nebraska. (1936)

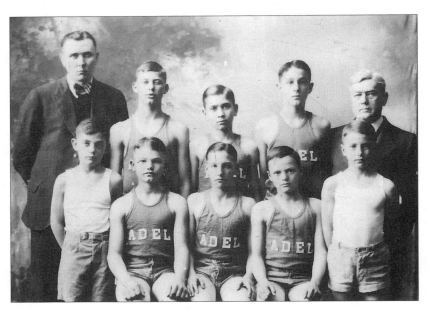

Nile (first row, lower left) with his coaches and Adel Junior High teammates. (1931)

Nile (center) coaching football at the park. (1940)

Nile, Frances, Ben, and George at home in Adel, Iowa. (1933)

The Way of Nile

The First Quarter,

Part Two

⌒

February 24

But we may be sure that if this great University in succeeding in her aims then we shall be successful in ours.

February 25

(A portion of Nile's 1940 Commencement speech) I prepared
this short talk several weeks ago but since then so many
events of terrible and ominous significance have taken
place in the world that I almost revised it. The bloody ho-
locaust raging in Europe with its possible repercussions in
this country tends to exert depressive influence on all of
us—and as a result many of you will scoff at many of my remarks as foolish hopes and mere fictions. However, whether
we know it or not, or like it or not, we in this country live by
idealistic hopes and by fictions. And it may be that in the
last analysis, these seeming fictions and idealisms will prove
to be the only realities. With this thought in mind I shall read
this speech with absolutely no apologies for the hopes and
aspirations expressed.

February 26

By now we should have learned that success and happiness and attainment come only periodically, not permanently—that they really are only passing moments in our experience—and that therein lies the explanation of the law of progress, and human dynamics.

February 27

(A portion of Nile's Heisman Trophy Award acceptance speech)... I'd like to make a comment which in my mind is indicative perhaps of the greater significance of football and sports emphasis in this country, and that is, I thank God I am warring on the gridirons of the Midwest and not on the battlefields of Europe. I can speak confidently and positively that the players of this country would much more, much rather, struggle and fight to win the Heisman Award than the Croix de Guerre...

February 28

Why the constant hurry and intensity of present day life? I suppose it is a result of... the general philosophy of "do" and then "do" some more, to accomplish, then start something else. The general idea seems to be that he who accomplishes the most, visibly and mentally, is closest to being the ideal man. Personally, I discount this viewpoint and fail to see the desirability or worth of...being on the "go" all the time.

February 29

We can accomplish much if we implement mental discipline and inspiration with real mental courage.

March 1

(A portion of Nile's 1940 Commencement speech) Tonight we seniors are gathered here as college graduates. Four short but dynamic years have gone fleeing by—it seems only yesterday that we entered this University as the very greenest of freshman. Each one of us has treated and experienced these four years in different ways. To some it has been one grand holiday at father's expense marred only by the necessity of a certain amount of study and classroom attendance; to others it has been a grand opportunity to fulfill the hopes and aspirations of posterity-minded parents, and to others a stern and intense experience—an opportunity, yes—but realized on only by treading the rough and rocky road of unmitigated hard work.

March 2

(A portion of Nile's 1940 Commencement speech)...regardless of what this college experience has meant to different students, this evening we stand as one body; and in a few days we shall stand together once more to receive that which is emblematic of four years of academic study well done—*our diploma.*

March 3

(A portion of Nile's 1940 Commencement speech) Some of us will treasure this scrap of paper, and some will be indifferent, and some will be cynical and unappreciative. But to all of us it will serve as a sort of "union card": hence forward, we are members of that group who have "been to college." Unfortunately, it can't honestly be said that we are now educated—but certainly, at least, this diploma indicates that we have been satisfactorily exposed to the process.

March 4

I am thankful for the blessings that are mine.

March 5

I guess I am just a little boy still. Sometimes I wonder if I am not just one of these nice guys whom the parents like & wish their children would emulate but doesn't seem to have much idea how to make a living.

March 6

But be that it may I know that we are full of ambition, courage, and a desire to do well for ourselves and for the society of which we are a part.

March 7

The battlefront is coming closer for us aviators. Almost before we know it we will be in the thick of it. Sometimes I wonder what it all means. But I know of no honorable course except ahead and through. May God be with me.

March 8

We are told on the one hand by the pedagogues of this University that the salvation of this nation is on our shoulders, and on the other hand depicted in the honorable Ding Darling's cartoons as naïve, intellectually doped youngsters without any ideas of practicality.

March 9

I speak of you courageous boys and girls unfavored by financial assistance from home who have earned your way by outside work on this campus; who have struggled desperately to meet your physical needs and at the same time maintain a decent classroom average—no social activities or frivolous pleasures have been yours—but you have asked for no quarter nor given any.

March 10

Are we capable of successfully meeting the problems that face us? Have we been adequately equipped to fulfill our manifest duties and obligations? Only time can honestly answer.

March 11

A great majority of our political and economic troubles arise from a lack of candor in our leaders. They try to be too smooth and adroit. They put partisan advantage above conviction.

March 12

We shall struggle to be sufficient unto the need—if it means better government we shall be active there, if it means a more enlightened business leadership we shall strive for that; and if it means a broader, more responsible international outlook, count on us to be alert and ready.

March 13

Fundamentally, all true education is composed of (1) mental discipline and (2) inspiration—And one is of no avail without the other. All successful teaching must hinge on these two necessary fundamentals.

March 14

Nobly have our professors endeavored to embody these principles in their lectures and personal associations with us. Hopefully, now they will watch our progress to see if we make use of the tools with which they have tried to provide us.

March 15

(*On December 3, 1941, Nile said this about going to war in a letter to his friend, Bob Hobbs*) It is too bad that a man has to leave things behind for military service, but what has to be done has to be done, I guess. I am not expecting to love the service, but on the other hand I am doing just exactly what I think I should do, there am leaving without any real regrets or backward glances.

March 16

I remember reading a letter that Washington wrote his mother right after his first battle…" I have heard the whistle of bullets past my ears and I have found it not unpleasant." Wonder what my first reaction will be?

March 17

We all seem to have the courage to face the physical forces of life—sickness, poverty, unemployment—even war itself—but how about courage of conviction, of morality, of idealism, courage of faith in a principle tangible proof of which is slow in appearing.

March 18

Herein lies that phrase of these problems which we must meet by ourselves, unaided by any university-given tools. Here is that angle of the greater difficulty which most often has proven the weak point in graduates of the past. True, we must learn to face adversity with equanimity, and even philosophically, but at the same time never for a moment losing sight of the ultimate goal, never failing in our ambition, or our ideals.

March 19

And what now—where do we go from here? Certainly, it isn't a very pretty picture—unemployment and uncertainty here at home and international anarchy abroad. What part are we to play in this dynamic ever changing world?

March 20

But you know and I know that this period of easy idealism is now at an end. And it is here that this other element of which I speak and which can be provided by the individual and the individual alone enters into the picture. I refer, fellow graduates, to a *real, positive, mental courage.*

March 21

However, the successful use of what we have learned here will be contingent entirely upon the addition of another element which we alone can provide. For whether we realize it or not we have lived a rather sheltered life here at The University; here our ideals are lauded, appreciated and protected—the development and expression of a social consciousness has been easy.

March 22

Injustice, oppression and war will ultimately bring on their own destruction—suffering and misery eventually awaken the human race. But that is the long sad, unenlightened road we have taken in the centuries past. Now is the time for these problems to be solved by enlightened thought and understanding.

March 23

...no longer can this country afford to have two parties whose avowed principle is always to stand for the exact opposite of the other regardless of what the stand is.

March 24

Our competitive urge must not only be objective but subjective, not only physical but spiritual.

March 25

The task is not easy—wishful thinking will not do the job— we shall have to battle until we seemingly have reached the end of the line, then "tie a knot" and "hang-on." (This is not just a figure of speech but an imperative necessity.)

March 26

So let us confidently take courage in what we deem to be right, and no matter what our line of endeavor may be, cling to its concomitants of persistence, desire, imagination, hope and faith.

March 27

Never have seen a place where the student officers so flagrantly take advantage of their positions—favoritism, partiality, drinking in their rooms—all wrong—but I'm afraid a bit typical of men hastily thrown into positions of some responsibility.

March 28

(A portion of Nile's 1940 commencement speech) You have been willing to pay the price for that which so many of us take as a matter of course; you hold your heads high tonight—and rightly so—for you have fought and won.

March 29

The feeling that politics and government is not the place for gentlemen has too long been accepted.

March 30

How happy we have been. Through thick and thin we have come and so it shall be. But let us not forget the struggle that is going on in the world today.

March 31

...I am afraid that there are too many who just come and admire and respect but aren't enthusiastically convinced enough to vote the right way.

Admiration

Chapter Two

This story will reveal my admiration for Nile Kinnick's accomplishments and the similar approaches we have shared in facing our challenges and adversities. Many of his quotes reflect some of the convictions, aspirations, and personal attributes that define who I am. For years, I have been intrigued by his thoughts and how they have connected to my life.

After reading and hearing about Nile's tremendous exploits on and off the football field in 1939, I was left with a crucial question that needed an answer. How could Nile be so spectacular and accomplish so much against some of the toughest teams in America? After all, Nile was only five feet eight inches tall and weighed just 170 pounds! This caused me to delve into my research. With great determination and curiosity, I pursued my interest in finding more details about this revered individual.

My earliest recollection and admiration for Kinnick and the 1939 Iowa football team began in 1964. I had just graduated from Iowa City High School in June of that year and began classes in the fall at The State University of Iowa (renamed The University of Iowa in 1964) as a seventeen-year-old freshman. During my first semester, I became aware of the fact that one of my Sigma Nu fraternity pledge brothers, Bill Green, Jr., was the son of Bill Green, Sr., a teammate of Nile Kinnick. Discovering that Green, Sr. and Kinnick played on that same 1939 Iowa football team known as the Ironmen was surprising and led to further conversations with my pledge brother about his dad and Kinnick.

Years later when Iowa Stadium was renamed Kinnick Stadium in 1972, I knew Nile was special, and my interest was rekindled once again. After all, it's remarkable to have the only stadium in the country named after a Heisman Trophy winner. My inquiry and curiosity searching for new facts about Nile led to astounding revelations. I was unaware that Nile played for three head coaches, Ossie Solem, Irl Tubbs, and Eddie Anderson, during his four years at Iowa. And, as a player on the 1937 and 1938 football teams, he and his teammates had only one victory over a Big Ten Conference team, the University of Chicago, who abolished their football program after the 1939 season. Those two football seasons had an overall record of 2-13-1 and a Big Ten record of 1-8-1. Even more dismal was the Hawkeye's record of winning only twenty-two games from 1930 through 1938. In five of those years they did not beat a Big Ten opponent. During the 1938 Iowa football season, the team did not score a touchdown in its last five games. Changes in the program had to be made.

No one anticipated that the 1939 football season was going to be special. A new coach was on the horizon and the search produced the next leader of Iowa's football team, Dr. Eddie Anderson. He arrived on the Iowa campus with great credentials from the College of the Holy Cross in Massachusetts where he accrued a winning record of 47-7-4 in six years. In a letter to his family in late November of that same year, Nile had this to say about the new direction Iowa was taking with the hiring of Anderson:

"Head Coach Anderson impressed me very favorably. Both he and I took an immediate liking & respect for each other I am quite confident.....I liked very much what he said in his speech yesterday and his quotations in the paper this morning. He talks as if he appreciates the athlete's viewpoint. I hope this proves true. He has a lot of fire and enthusiasm and looks to be a very determined man."

This unbreakable 1939 football team ended the season nearly winning the Big Ten Championship. The leadership of Eddie Anderson and Nile Kinnick was recognized by fans and writers everywhere. The Iowa squad ended the season with a 6-1-1 win-loss record, placed second in the Big Ten, and was ranked 9th in the Nation in the final AP Poll. Anderson was even named National Coach of the Year.

Anderson had a mutual respect and admiration for Nile and years later said:

"Nile Kinnick was the greatest football player I have ever coached and one of the greatest and most courageous I have ever seen. They named me Coach of the Year in 1939,

but there is no doubt that the glory belonged to Iowa and Kinnick."

Nile and Dr. Eddie were obviously the foundation of this acclaimed and successful team. Many writers and fans said this scanty squad of players achieved the impossible and were a team for the ages. Yet, many of these athletes played on the same Iowa team the previous two years without much success. Even more remarkable during this 1939 campaign, was that thirteen players played the entire sixty minutes of at least one game!

George "Red" Frye, now deceased, was a football player I met several years ago at FRYfest, an event named after Hayden Fry, one of the greatest Hawkeye coaches of all time. "Red" mentioned to me in a conversation that in the last game of the 1939 season, when Iowa tied Northwestern 6-6, he became an Ironman by playing an entire sixty-minute game both offensively and defensively. He told me that he was the last player to become one of the thirteen Ironmen on that 1939 Iowa team.

Kinnick was one of those Ironmen, too. According to Iowa records, this modest and unassuming Ironman played every minute in six straight games. He ended the season playing 402 consecutive minutes which included the first forty-two minutes in the game against Northwestern. Then Nile had to leave the game due to a separated shoulder. Kinnick was involved in sixteen of Iowa's nineteen touchdowns either by rushing or by passing and was responsible for 107 of the 130 points scored during the season. Nile also broke fourteen school records during that year! His achievements were rewarded by receiving consensus First-Team All-American, Big Ten MVP, All-Big Ten status, the Walter Camp Memorial Trophy, and the Maxwell Award. A man of small stature won almost every prestigious award possible including the Heisman Memorial Trophy awarded yearly to the most outstanding college football player in America. Nile's performance exemplified what this award represents, the "pursuit of excellence with integrity." Heisman recipients "demonstrate great ability on the football field combined with diligence, perseverance, and hard work." Nile's achievements were the reason this "rags to riches" team went beyond preseason predictability. With a determined effort, he led his team to achieve the impossible.

My admiration for Nile stemmed from his being a tenacious competitor with an indomitable spirit to play entire games and prevail through injuries. Nile dealt with several unfortunate injuries during his college football career including a serious ankle injury, possibly bruised ribs, a separated shoulder, and numerous other ailments. And, I'm sure, there were also academic challenges to keep his grades at a high level in the classroom. But Kinnick had the mental fortitude to push on and the will to never give up no matter how difficult the situation.

Occasionally, some of Nile's written thoughts were about battling adversities, having the attitude to be the best he could be on the football field and in the classroom, and accepting challenges. After reading several of his entries, I began to identify with one of Kinnick's brilliantly written and captivating insights. Nile once said: "...we must learn to face adversity with equanimity, and even philosophically, but at the same time never for a moment losing sight of the ultimate goal, never failing in our ambition, or our ideals."

To be honored and accomplish so much, I feel that Nile was a man of multiple "FITNESSES." In many of Nile's insights that I documented while researching, were examples of quotes relating to what I refer to as: *spiritual fitness, mental fitness, physical fitness,* and *social fitness.* I call these four fitnesses a "Quadrant of Life," a philosophy I developed during a difficult life-changing four-month period in August of 2016. Daily, I relied heavily on these fitnesses to help me cope with my diagnosis of a rare plasma cell cancer. I sensed that this was going to be the biggest challenge I had ever encountered and would become the most difficult time in my life. Facing this diagnosis was not an easy task, but like Kinnick, I persevered, stayed positive, and made the best of a bad situation. A person is never too old to have a role model.

To improve my *spiritual fitness* in my "Quadrant of Life," I turned to God to strengthen my faith and give me hope. Worshiping God and participating in small group Bible studies were examples of many of the positive distractions I used on a daily basis to confront my struggles. Through prayer and scripture, I asked God to come into my life to give me guidance and comfort.

Nile seemed to have faith in God, too, and to be spiritually fit based on some of the entries in his diaries. About the Bible, Nile said…"best of all a spiritual understanding of its inspired word will bring the same comfort and healing that it did in the early days of Christianity." He also commented that the Bible… "is a practical teaching and its application is sorely needed in the world today." Nile understood that being disciplined, having compassion for others, modeling integrity to the best of our abilities, and retaining humility and dependence on our faith in God reaps great rewards.

The second fitness in my "Quadrant of Life" was also essential. My *mental fitness* helped me to cope and face my illness by maintaining a good healthy attitude. When I was uncomfortable,

I avoided negativity by changing thoughts within myself. I continued my research and writing of this book and stayed abreast of current events. These tasks helped me face my new reality and kept me moving forward. Like Nile, having a desire to read, learn, and understand various topics was helpful in strengthening my mental fitness to battle adversities and to never give up.

Some statements written in a final letter to Nile's parents demonstrated his mental fitness. He said:

"The task which lies ahead is adventure as well as duty, and I am anxious to get at it. I feel better in mind and body than I have in ten years, and am quite certain that I can meet the foe confident and unafraid."

Those comments were an example of Nile's approach to going into war to serve his country. Nile also said about competition, "Have you ever learned to compete? Work hard and keep going when it isn't easy."

The third fitness I formulated in my "Quadrant of Life" was *physical fitness*. Being a passionate and intense person, I worked hard to be positive and persevere through my serious health issues. I knew I had a rocky road of medical problems ahead of me, so in November of 2016, five weeks before the end of my chemotherapy, I was determined to train and compete in an indoor triathlon.

On January 27, 2017, with a "you-can-do-it" attitude, I, like Nile, was determined to be the best I could be to achieve my goal. In the men's competition, after the overall winners were announced, I won my age bracket and three other age brackets by swimming in a pool, cycling on a spinner bike, and running on a treadmill.

Being active, working out in my local athletic club to maintain strength, cardiovascular and core fitness, and doing yard work and other physical tasks were important to keep my body strong. In addition, traveling, attending sporting events, concerts, and plays were my solutions to maintain a healthy attitude and continue on a positive path of fitness.

An example of Nile's physical fitness was in a letter he wrote to his parents before the historic 1939 football season. Anticipating the new football coach and staff's arrival on the Iowa campus and preparation for the fall campaign, Kinnick said:

> *"For three years, nay for fifteen years, I have been preparing for this last year of football. The season just passed has removed much of the tension that might have attended this last effort. I feel confident and free from the pressure of 'absolutely necessary success' and falsely accepted responsibility. I anticipate becoming the roughest, toughest, all-around back yet to hit this conference. That is a little strong, of course, but nevertheless I am not planning to be robbed of my consummation."*

When Nile wrote this, he knew the intense training and sacrifice he had to endure. That was a commitment, not a feeling.

In spite of injuries, Kinnick stayed on course during the 1939 football season and accomplished his goal. By being the "roughest, toughest all-around back" in the Conference, Nile won the Big Ten Most Valuable Player award by the widest margin of votes ever. Nile also received Male Athlete of the Year voted on by the Associated Press sports editors across the country. Kinnick was the first amateur to win this award, beating out legendary professional athletes Joe Dimaggio, New York Yankee slugger, and Joe Lewis, world heavyweight boxing champion!

Last, but not the least of the four "FITNESSES" is *social fitness*. To me, it was vital to be around family and friends who were positive in their thoughts and who loved and supported me through prayer. Attending social events, being involved in volunteer work, and serving others were priorities. Kinnick once said, "Consideration and helpfulness are great virtues and well worth cultivating."

All of these fitnesses helped me become a stronger person, more determined, and more positive, much like Nile who faced adversities with strength and courage. This "Quadrant of Life" continues to help me cope with and accept life's "ups and downs," and all the surprises you do not anticipate. I believe Nile had a similar philosophy of life going through his challenges as a student-athlete and an ensign in the Naval Air Corps Reserve.

Kinnick was an honorable, considerate, compassionate, and respectable man. His work ethic and self-discipline were beyond reproach on the field and in the classroom. Being the courageous competitor he was and serving his country so bravely, there was no question he was worthy of my attention. My connection was there; my interest peaked; my admiration soared.

The Way of Nile

The Second Quarter,

Part One

April 1

Two civilizations are at stake—Truth and error are at bay—and Truth will come thru triumphantly thru us daily affirming for ourselves and all the absolute supremacy of Truth, Life and Love—the utter inability of any anti-Christ, materialism, mesmerism to shackle man or to do battle against God.

April 2

Each year brings new blessings upon our family. The success of one is the success of all and the problem of one is shared by each of us.

April 3

Portentous times are these and we are sluggards in the race if we do not [do] our part mentally to the best of our ability.

April 4

How well I have taken advantage of the football reputation it was my good fortune to gain is for others to judge, but I personally am very thankful for the whole experience and the fun and friends it has brought me.

April 5

Lincoln was a moral and upright man. He was a pacifist at heart. But when there was no other alternative he did not equivocate nor cravenly talk of peace when there was no peace.

April 6

Men will choose wisely if they can choose freely.

April 7

(About Lincoln) He grabbed the bull by the horns; realizing that the nation could not endure half slave and half free, he threw down the gauntlet and eradicated the evil. We are faced with the same thing and the longer we wait the worse it becomes.

April 8

May God give me the courage to do my duty and not falter. This isn't a dramatic speech—it is honestly the way I feel.

April 9

By golly, I have had a good time at this base, have met a lot of mighty good acquaintances, learned to fly to a degree, and still have had time to get out a little now and then. Once again I say that my football and college experience in general has been excellent training for this period of my life.

Being constantly on the go, getting cussed out frequently, keeping going when you're tired, none of these are novel experiences for a college football player. And I am glad I got my studies quite well as I went along…making things infinitely more easy for me now.

April 10

I expect I would rather be able to write well and speak well than anything I can think of. A well written and well delivered speech on something of import gives me a bigger thrill than just about anything.

April 11

A man who talks but is afraid to act, who sacrifices principle to expediency whenever real danger threatens is not worthy to keep and enjoy what he has.

April 12

It is very sobering to realize just what the future holds for a boy my age. On the other hand it is a practical challenge to a man's courage and personal integrity.

April 13

I have spoken before of the wonderful heritage which you and Grandpa have given all the grandchildren. It is All-American in every way—morally, physically, and mentally, I know that each of us realizes that whatever his achievement may be that it in a large measure stems from this background.

April 14

I have intimated that I believe reading and writing and speaking to be the very essence of an education (Figuring or computation should be included also.) I believe this because an effort to excel in each of these develops a disciplined mind and demands orderly thought and expression.

April 15

He is not worthy of his background and heritage who kowtows to tyranny in order to cling to his temporary safety and comfort. This is no expression of oratory or emotionalism but cold, hard truth.

April 16

I trust I will have the courage to act as I speak come what may. It will not be easy—but *should*, therefore, can be done.

April 17

When I listen to Churchill give his incomparable speeches I can hardly remain seated in my chair. What frankness, what defiance, and yet withal what inspiration is in each utterance. May we all prove worthy of the cause he is espousing in the trying times ahead.

April 18

(A Bible verse from Psalm 16:8 that Nile used in his last letter to his parents) "I have set the Lord always before me, because He is at my right hand, I shall not be moved."

April 19

Some of the boys may be living just from day to day with a fatalism precluding plans for the future. Not I—my imagination goes beyond the war to those blessed days of peace which will one day come again.

April 20

...when it comes to writing a man must have some opportunity to practice in order to improve. None of my courses seem to provide a satisfactory outlet for the practice I need. I want to learn to set down my ideas clearly and plainly and withal develop some beauty and power of expression. Thus far the best that I do is to record what disorderly [idea?] comes to my mind.

April 21

What we need are men of greater stature & character in congress.

April 22

The poor colored people are kicked from pillar to post, condemned, cussed, ridiculed, accorded no respect, permitted no sense of human dignity. What can be done I don't know. Nearly everyone, particularly the southerners, seem to think the only problem involved is seeing to it that they keep their place, whatever that may be.

April 23

(Nile's hyperbole)…the moon was the greatest wonder of it all. Round and full no clouds contested her light, even the stars kept a respective distance. She was queen of the night, lovely pure, unapproachable, undisputed sovereign of the celestial realm. Soft and silvery was her light, bathing all below in gentle benediction.

April 24

Oh, for the farm where a man is truly independent, and where he deals with fundamentals, where the changing seasons brings changed work, and a man is out-of-doors all the time.

April 25

It is on the farm that a man can devote his life to his investment and see the improvement and growth from year to year.

April 26

In the interest of justice and public welfare I agree that a gov't should stand by as a benevolent sheriff, alert and on the job, but I am suspicious of any extension of that power.

April 27

As long as an administration is definitely prejudiced in favor of labor regardless of the circumstances of the case, business has little opportunity to prove that it could solve the unemployment problem.

April 28

When Congress passes a law demanding judicial settlement of disputes between labor and its bosses as well as between labor and capital, we shall have started on the right road.

April 29

I decided to see the movie In *Which We Serve*. It was excellent and deserving of all the fine things which have been said about it. I guess I'm a sucker for depictions of courage, honor, duty, devotion to home and country—my eyes were wet half the time.

April 30

Whenever this administration, or some other, becomes more impartial as between labor and capital this union mess will begin to clear up.

May 1

(About Franklin D. Roosevelt) If the old time virtues of private resourcefulness and thrift, adherence to principle, governmental economy, intellectual & political honesty are of no importance, then Franklin has had scarcely any fault as a president.

May 2

Give a man one close friend, tried and true, and he is fortified against the world; make that friend a woman and there are no heights he cannot scale.

May 3

In my mind any extension of gov't control in this country is particularly bad, for the simple reason that we, as a people, do not yet take pride in government positions; they are almost positions of contempt in our eyes.

May 4

It really pains me to see the farm interests making every effort to crack the existing price structure, for farmers mean IOWA to me, and I want always to be proud of her and what she stands for.

May 5

It is vitally important that everyone from electorate through the political parties up to the nominees themselves, measure up to the highest concepts of statesmanship.

May 6

The changing season of the Midwest—the intense heat in the summer, bitter cold in the winter, and unsurpassable beauty and invigorating weather of fall and spring—is what makes it an interesting place to live. Only robust and virile people can live in such a climate and enjoy it.

May 7

Surely it is such thoughts and deeds which flicker from out the night of hatred and strife that promise the certainty of mankind's true brotherhood.

May 8

(After hearing and seeing Marian Anderson sing at the Metropolitan Opera House in New York City) Her powerful, heartfelt rendition of *Sometimes I Feel Like a Motherless Child* was marvelous. I could hear the moan and wail of the Negro soul echoing through the centuries…The perfection of her tone and interpretation swelled out over her listeners and we all closed our eyes and felt as if we were in church.

May 9

There are too many Americans who don't yet appreciate the real value of liberty & freedom of enterprise. If the gov't continues to "take over" more & more who is going to be the arbiter in any complaints and disputes which arise? The tyranny and abuses of business and labor will then be present in the government itself and doubly hard to correct.

May 10

(A letter to his father in 1943) Your response to my thought that we might someday combine our talents for mutual profit and enjoyment made me very happy. You as farm production manager and I as a warrior in the political field, frequently returning to the country homestead for encouragement and strength has the most appeal. However, let's keep our minds and eyes open for any opportunity of whatever nature—and which could include the whole family. Among the five of us we have a good combination of health, energy, ambition, brains, talent, industry. It would be so much fun to capitalize on it to the benefit of all.

May 11

We either must jump in this mess strongly regardless of the risk or refuse to take our rightful place in the world. More than at any time since the Napoleonic period Western Civilization and Christianity are at stake. That puts it strongly but is no exaggeration just the same.

May 12

Soon the countryside will be green...and, yes, the grass will be a grab and a half high, and picnics will displace the afternoon schedule.

May 13

It is important that every member of the family grow and look forward all the time.

May 14

We are not people apart; there is no reason in the world why we shouldn't fight for the preservation of a chance to live freely; no reason why we shouldn't suffer to uphold that which we want to endure then it is anyone else. And it is a matter of self-preservation right this very minute. Those are my sentiments—and they are RIGHT.

May 15

Whenever we go, whatever we do, I know that our minds shall frequently flood with tender memories of the hearthside and with happy plans for the day when law and peace shall reign once again.

Photographs
Student-Athlete

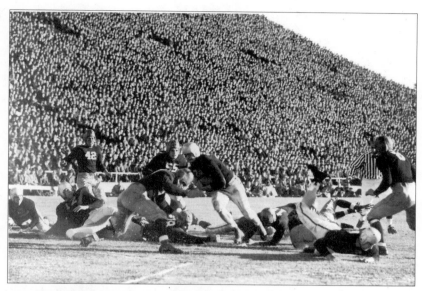

Kinnick scoring a touchdown to take the lead against Notre Dame, 6-0.

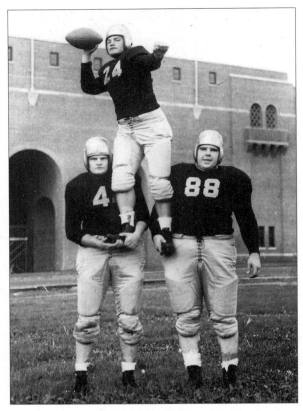

Wally Bergstrom and Henry Luebeke, linemen, holding Nile Kinnick at a photo shoot in front of Iowa Stadium.

Sisters, Mary Jane Walsh (left) and Catherine Walsh (right) both from Davenport, Iowa, walk arm-in-arm with Nile at the Downtown Athletic Club in New York City. (December, 1939)

Nile receiving the Heisman Trophy award for the most outstanding college football player in America.

Frank Carideo, backfield coach for Iowa, watching Kinnick's punting technique during practice.

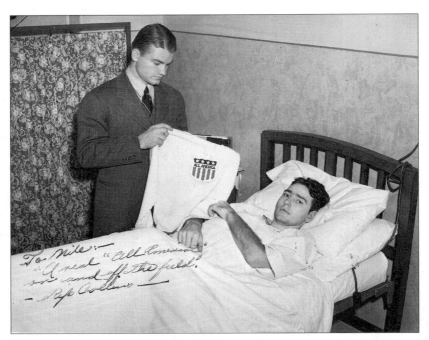

Kinnick presenting his All-American sweater to Edwin "Rip" Collins, a New Jersey high school football player, three days after he had his leg amputated from a game injury. (December 10, 1939)

Nile with his maternal grandmother, Arletta Clarke, wife of George W. Clarke, Govenor of Iowa from 1913 to 1917. (March, 1940)

Nile on the cover of the 1940 All-Star Football Game program at Soldier Field in Chicago.

Kinnick posing on the practice field. (1939)

Nile at Benson High School in Omaha, Nebraska, refining his punting skills. (Summer, 1939)

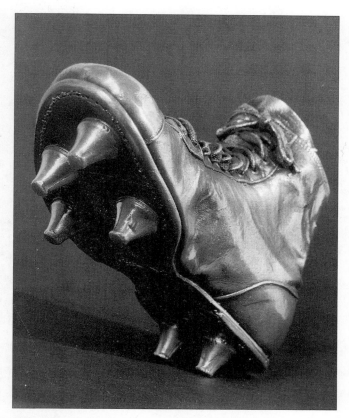

Nile Kinnick's bronzed football shoe. (1939)

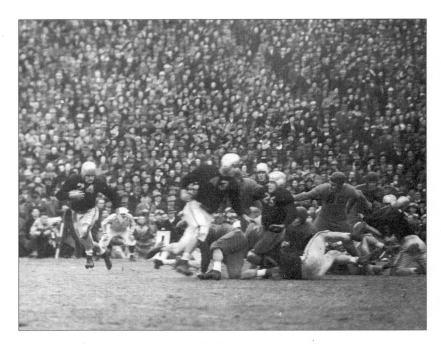

Nile, 24, carrying the ball during the Minnesota game. Number 43 is Bill Green, Sr. Iowa won on a pass from Kinnick to Green, 13-9. (November 18, 1939)

Kinnick, sophomore, played basketball at Iowa and was the second leading scorer on the team.

Nile Kinnick with bust of himself, sculpted by Dora Mason.

Dora Mason, a long-time Iowa City resident, earned her master's degree in sculpture from The State University of Iowa in 1938. Her most famous live sculpture was of Nile Kinnick just before he graduated and shortly after he received the Heisman trophy in 1940. Nile and Dora had become friends over time by walking to their respective homes together. Nile had seen a bust of his grandfather George W. Clark, a former governor of Iowa in the statehouse. He hoped some day that he would merit the honor to be like his grandfather. While Nile studied for an exam, Dora studied him and sculpted the bust out of clay, later to be cast in bronze. (Caption provided by Rich Mason)

Nile, No. 24, carrying the ball against Notre Dame. (November 11, 1939)

Nile with his mother, father, and Coach Eddie Anderson (far right), Iowa's head football coach.

At the Downtown Athletic Club in New York City, Nile is presented with the Heisman Trophy.

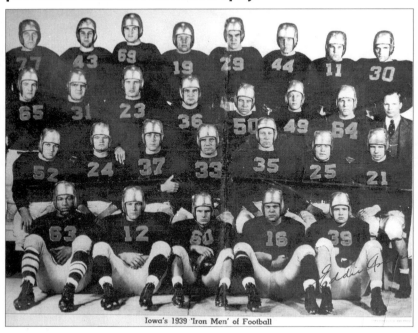

Iowa's 1939 'Iron Men' of Football

Iowa's 1939 Ironmen team photo.

Kinnick signing autographs for his young fans.

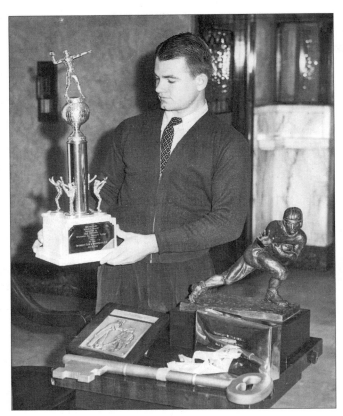

Nile holding his Walter Camp Memorial Trophy.

Football team captain Irwin Prasse giving Kinnick the game ball after Iowa defeated nationally ranked Notre Dame, 7-6.

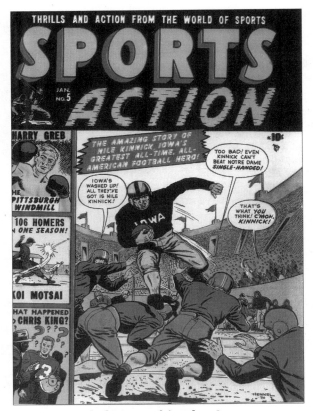

Nile Kinnick featured in the January, 1951 edition comic book, *Sports Action*.

The Way of Nile
The Second Quarter,
Part Two

May 16

All this will be easy, even that which you don't care for particularly, if you maintain & broaden your sense of humor and stick by your BOOKS.

May 17

Truly we have shared to the full life, love, and laughter. Comforted in the knowledge that your thought and prayer go with us every minute, and sure that your faith and courage will never falter no matter the outcome, I bid you *au revoir*.

May 18

(*One of Nile's favorite quotes from Longfellow*)
"Not enjoyment, not sorrow
Is our destined end or way.
But to act that each tomorrow
Find us farther than today."
I think I like Longfellow best of all the American poets. He is always simple and easy to understand and writes sentiments and situations dear to my heart.

May 19

I cannot refrain from making this little observation. We have six toilets arranged so that three face each other for about 110 men…I do not have many aristocratic learnings, but, for some reason or another, I do like privacy when assuming the undignified position necessary for a bowel movement.

May 20

Barrack life is quite tolerable, but hardly a place in which I would want to bring up Lord Fauntleroy.

May 21

Our home and family life has been grand and fruitful, and it will be even better after this war is over. All that we have been or shall be we boys owe to your affection, discipline, and guidance.

May 22

(*Portion of Nile's final letter to his parents*) The task which lies ahead is adventure as well as duty, and I am anxious to get at it. I feel better in mind and body than I have for ten years, and am quite certain that I can meet the foe confident and unafraid.

May 23

…we must eternally seek those laws & institutions which will most readily implement our ideals & reduce to a minimum the conditions tempting the frailties of human nature.

May 24

(*About squadron mate, Bill Reiter, his wife, and another couple*)
And after dinner we sat around the fireplace talking and
listening to the radio. How comfortable it all was—the girls
knitting sweaters and sox for their adored spouses and they
lounging around in their 'sand-crab' clothes (civvies to you).
Those early years of married life must be divine—ah my,
someday perhaps, I too shall experience those blessings.

May 25

(*Last letter Nile wrote was to his friend, Celia Peairs*) Am so
glad you could speak enthusiastically of your visit in Iowa
City. That little town means so much to me—the scene of
growth and development during vital years—joy and mel-
ancholy, struggle, and triumph. It is almost like home. I love
the people, the campus, the trees, everything about it. And
it is beautiful in the spring. Ah, for those days of laughter
and picnics when the grass was newly green.

May 26

(*After a military weekend "liberty" in New York City*) I had a
fine time, but I was alone; and happiness unshared is like
a picture without those colors that give it, warmth and
meaning.

May 27

(*A portion of a letter Nile wrote to his father*) Heretofore,
mother has, for the most part, done the counseling, advis-
ing, etc. Of course you always sat in judgment with her...

However the time has come when you must be the protagonist. I feel that many quiet discussions between you and me are necessarily imminent; I look forward to them.

May 28

Appeared before Marine Selection Board …unhappily, selection was determined by lottery…disappointed at the time, but now don't regret it at all…lottery rather than merit…that branch loses most of its appeal for me.

May 29

As a result of the nationwide commercialization of sport and development of the win-at-any-price attitude there is apt to develop dubious tactics and an unhealthy outlook toward the game by players and coaches alike…However, to the boy who looks for the sheer fun of healthy competition, who is motivated by a desire that the best man win, and that the laws of honesty and fair play shall obtain…to him the game may prove of worth, though it be corrupted and controlled.

May 30

(*One of Nile's favorite quotes by Wendell Willkie*):

"How can you ever have political & econ. Freedom where the state owns everything."

Am proud of Willke and disgusted with the majority of the Republican Party—they better snap out of it or they won't be anymore. Some sort of parliamentary system will eventually show up out of this.

May 31

Where the white man's pocketbook & social & racial superiority is involved his humanitarian impulses are quick to recede.

June 1

You know, at best, eating is an ungraceful activity. But when 8 or 10 men are rapidly partaking of their sustenance at the same table it is some sight. Usually 4 men or so are facing each other as they eat. It brings back memories of my days on the farm as I watched the porkers get their feeding. I have noted that some of the most dignified officers lose all semblance of superior rank or excellence of movement while eating. Knowing of my own shortcoming in this art, I grieve to think of the impression I must give.

June 2

(*About military training*) A man must have patience around here. Everything is extremely impersonal. It will be a real test for my character and temperament. It is the first time in a good long time that I haven't had an immediate opportunity to show my full ability. I must qualify that—law school presented a similar situation, but the service tops even that experience for difficulty of recognition.

June 3

...take a deep breath, stick out my chin and persevere until the skies clear again.

June 4

(*A portion of a letter written to his parents about the changes he wanted to make about his grades, ankle injury, and overall campus life-style before the fall semester*) Truth crushed to earth will rise again. If I could confront you now I believe you would say, 'My how well you look and act.' And I do feel fine, exuberant, expectant.

June 5

Where there is a duty or dangerous job to be done a good leader is the first to volunteer.

June 6

Sometimes this war looks to be an interminable mess.

June 7

...Finished Steinbeck's *Grapes of Wrath*. It is a course in language and episode, but realistic and a tough protest against an unjust situation. The humor was rough but good—I laughed a lot.

June 8

It is a glorious spring day. Some of the boys are knocking out flies and some are just basking in the sun. It makes one want to breathe deeply and be happy he is alive.

June 9

Too often in a military organization leadership is gained through seniority or political appointment and not merit itself. Superimposed leadership is seldom successful.

June 10

Truly nothing stirs the imagination of red-blooded youth like the prospect of battle.

June 11

Seems as if I have been hurrying all my life. Gets kind of old sometimes.

June 12

This failure to work together, to compromise, to recognize merit in others, this small mind pettiness seems to be a historical characteristic of government and military men. Inexcusable!

June 13

For two weeks I did everything but fly. The highest I ever got into the air was a top bunk.

June 14

This is Flag Day, I believe, and Old Glory really means more to us & to all the world at any other time in U.S. history. May we carry that grand banner to complete victory and soon.

June 15

This war is apt to be long, costly, bloody beyond any anticipation—all because of lack of foresight the world over. When will we learn!

June 16

There may have been a time when I was in love with love—but no more. However, I shall not consider my mortal existence complete until I have loved and won a woman who commands my admiration and respect in every way.

June 17

I now find myself moved strongly by feats of courage and battle heroism as depicted in such movies as *They Died with their Boots On*. I find myself anxious to do the same, to engage the enemy, and to comport myself with outstanding skill and daring.

June 18

(*To his father on Father's day*) Hello Gus: For you we wish you a happy Father's Day…You know, pop, these Father's Days come and go (I've wished you well for about twenty, I guess) and yet each year this day bids more eagerly than ever for us to express in some small way our love for you and what you mean to us. May twenty times twenty more Father's Days appear and find you the same, tender father, Gus.

June 19

…with no other alternative available I consistently find myself sitting on a cold stool opposite some lugubrious faced co-student & surrounded by waiting aspirants. If I have painted a relatively clear picture you will agree with me that such a situation is the epitome of the lowest form of democratic relationship among men.

June 20

Some personal dislikes follow: affectation, undue display of emotion of some kind, haughtiness, common argument full of absolute certainty excluding all other opinion or possibility.

June 21

(*About his military training*) At the beginning of one [of] our manuals is Kipling's poem "If" with the following line underscored—"if you can wait without being tired by waiting." Well, brother Kipling I can't; not anymore—I'm plenty tired with waiting—and if you wouldn't be "you are a better man than I, Gunga Din!!"

June 22

People must come before profits!!

June 23

It is a bit difficult to reconcile myself to the petty detail to which I am assigned all too frequently. Here I have had four years of regular college work & a year of law, and yet today I was picking up cigarette butts around the ad building like a common snipe hunter. I do not actually rebel at such duty, but now & then a bit of humorous cynicism sneaks into my thought.

June 24

Regardless of the degree of our civilization, people still thrill to physical combat & admire the man who excels.

June 25

A man is frequently lonely who has not become strongly attached to a fine woman by the time he is 23. I am not going into this war with the idea of losing my life, but, nonetheless I could more easily face the obvious risk if I were deeply in love with a clean, wholesome girl in the bloom of young womanhood.

June 26

If a man would grow in character his battle with self must be unceasing.

June 27

He who is of proven merit in the field of major sports has shown to all that he is possessed of strength, vigor, stamina, and courage. The great majority of people want to know such a man.

June 28

What that man does with such an opportunity to make friends depends on his common sense, his character, his temperament, and his sense of proportion.

June 29

Have now finished Tolstoy's monumental work...Found it enjoyable...His range of interest and knowledge seem illimitable and he can so simply describe a scene or character.

June 30

Dramatic contests give unity & stability to social organizations. War is a primitive type, & games (football) & judicial trial are civilized examples.

Inspiration

Chapter Three

Nile Kinnick approached his trials and tribulations with courage, faith, and patience. He balanced his studies, athletics, football injuries, law school, and coaching with a perpetually positive attitude. He accepted his accomplishments with humbleness and graciousness. Nile was able to endure physical and mental hardships. His challenges as an athlete and ensign in the US Naval Air Corps Reserve required a strength of mind that enabled him to encounter adversity and unforeseen danger with courage. The thoughts of Kinnick that you have read so far help tell his story.

Nile's insights had inspired me to continue my quest for a more accurate and deeper understanding of him. One of my favorite quotes came from his last military journal on June 1, 1943, the day before he died, when he was forced to land his Wildcat fighter plane in the Caribbean Sea. I carried this quote in my billfold for years and years when I was an elementary teacher, and referred to it from time to time. Nile said:

> *"It is a sad mistake to try and be the head man in every-thing you attempt. The axiom, if it's worth doing at all, it's worth doing well has its limitations. Stay on the ball most of the time, but learn to coast between moments of all-out effort."*

This quote reminded me that, on occasion, I needed to slow down, take a deep breath during my teaching, but stay "on the ball most of the time."

As a student at The University of Iowa in the mid-sixties, my major was Elementary Education. After graduating in 1969, my wife and I were hired to teach in Cedar Rapids, Iowa. During my first year of teaching I was shocked when drafted into the US Army during the Vietnam War. After my discharge in 1972, I was hired to teach in the Iowa City Community School District. Twenty-two of my thirty-one years of teaching, I specialized in developmental reading and worked with students both individually and in small groups. Being trained at The University of Iowa as an early reading intervention specialist or Reading Recovery teacher, I particularly loved the challenging and rewarding experience teaching disadvan-taged first graders who were at-risk of failure in reading. Diagnostic reading tests revealed many of my six or seven-year-old students were behind their peers in reading. Teaching these early readers the skills and strategies they needed to get them to read at their grade level or above was my goal. The task proved difficult with many of these students, but Nile's quote to "Stay on the ball most of the time, but learn to coast between moments of all-out effort" reminded me to take a deep breath, relax a little bit and focus on the importance of my job. Helping my students avoid being tracked into a learning disabilities program, and teaching them how to become independent and automatic processors of print was paramount.

Having Kinnick as a role model is a blessing to me because of his passion, character, values, and outlook on life. I find Nile especially inspiring because of our shared Iowa upbringing and the work ethic both of our parents modeled for us. Nile was a serious, persistent, and intense man. I was, too, and still am. He was goal-oriented with strong convictions. He had a "staying power" not to give up on arduous tasks, a resolve to find solutions, and the diligence to be thorough.

My research of Nile allowed me to better understand his personality over the years and inspired me to volunteer at The University of Iowa Athletics Hall of Fame and Museum (HOF). In July of 2002, one month after I retired, I received a telephone call that had a tremendous impact on my life. The call came from Robert A. Stein, National Iowa Varsity Club President and Hawkeye Ambassadors' Coordinator. Stein, both a graduate and recipient of a varsity letter in swimming at The State University of Iowa, asked me if I would be interested in serving as a Hawkeye Ambassador for the HOF opening in the fall of 2002. Having grown up in Iowa City, attended the public schools, received both my undergraduate and graduate degrees at The University of Iowa, I was more than thrilled and didn't hesitate to accept this volunteer position. I felt I was qualified to share my Hawkeye experiences and knowledge with visitors touring the HOF.

During the past sixteen years as a Hawkeye Ambassador, I have been involved in numerous projects at the HOF. One unique project was the opportunity to restore Nile Kinnick's Walter Camp Memorial Trophy given annually to the collegiate football player of the year. In 2003, prior to the restoration project, Joshua Larsen, a graduate assistant for the athletic department, delivered a cardboard box of vintage trophies to the recently opened Hall of Fame and Museum for display or storage. While I was sitting at the greeters' table, Larsen asked me what needed to be done with the old trophies. I said I would take the trophies to the basement for safe keeping. When Josh left, I looked in the box to see what the items were. Many were small, but probably significant trophies that were won by student-athletes decades ago. There were also loose trophy parts and pieces that were broken from some of the trophies' bases.

A few of the loose trophy parts, in particular, caught my attention. They were statuettes. After examining them more closely, I discovered that the pieces were part of a "puzzle" necessary to reconstruct, what turned out to be, Nile Kinnick's Walter Camp Trophy. What amazed me was that all of the pieces to the trophy were still in the box. None of the broken statuettes were missing after sixty-three years when Kinnick had received the award in 1940! I suspect the trophy had been set aside for repairs sometime in the past and then lost in the shuffle while moving it from place to place for safe keeping.

The brass nameplate was discolored and hard to read, but I was able to determine what some of the letters were and realized that this was, in fact, Nile Kinnick's trophy. The four "punting pose" statuettes that were previously mounted on the base of the trophy and the "quarterback throwing pose" at the very top of the trophy were horizontally broken at the ankles. There was an attempt to place a small steel rod in the ankle and upper leg of one of the statuettes, but the rod did not secure the two parts of the statuette.

I was told that replacing the statuettes would diminish the value and authenticity of the trophy. Also, the trophy shop's estimate for repair was very expensive. Liking a challenge, I offered to take this project on myself and attempt to restore this piece of memorabilia to its original condition. My goal was to have the trophy placed in the display case next to Kinnick's Heisman Trophy in the HOF filling in more of the history of Nile.

It goes without saying that I had no experience taking on such a delicate and time-consuming project, but I felt that if I didn't, there was a possibility that this piece of Hawkeye history might never be properly shared. Something had to be done, so getting the necessary permission, I gathered up the broken trophy pieces and transported them to my house. I felt a bit elated. Being a Hawkeye sports fan, having the Walter Camp Trophy in my car seemed unreal.

I spent the first few weeks of this three-month project contemplating what materials, tools, and procedures I would use for each step of the restoration. When I decided to use the family room as my workshop, my wife wasn't too thrilled at first, but she knew how important this project was to me and finally agreed.

After planning my steps and procedures, I was ready to begin. I decided to use a suitable, archival-quality adhesive to bond the upper and lower pieces of each of the five statuettes. It was a tricky, tedious, and time-consuming process since each of the statuettes was broken horizontally at the ankles. It was similar to someone taking a sharp knife and making a clean cut through each of the ankles. The welding agent took a minimum of fifteen hours to adhere properly and many times the leg of the statuette would gradually slide a tiny fraction of an inch. I would have to constantly observe for slippage, and when there was movement, I would start over again trying to adjust and fixate the upper and lower portions of the statuette.

My goal was to have no noticeable errors by the completion of the welding process and be sure the ankles were perfectly matched. To accomplish this and obtain balance, I experimented by sitting in a corner of our house with my back reinforced by the walls. I held the two pieces of the statuette firmly together waiting for the bonding agent to set. Unfortunately, when I would barely move, the upper and lower parts of the leg would separate. It took me awhile, but I finally realized this method would not work. I ended up using a small vice, bookends, and various knickknacks from our family room, such as magazines, notepads, books, and a screwdriver to secure and balance each statuette to complete the drying stage.

Once the statuette was dry and secure, I began the buffing and shaping stage using a rotary hand tool to remove the excess welding agent around the ankle area. This was a very delicate process requiring a gentle touch with minimal amounts of pressure. Once this step was completed, the antiquing stage began. I used my fingers to rub in a gold leaf finish on each statuette to avoid the look of brush strokes.

When the project was finally completed, the trophy, in my opinion, looked just like the original in the 1940 photograph I have of Nile holding his Walter Camp Trophy.

I did have a final setback before transporting the trophy back to the HOF. After placing it carefully in the front seat of my vehicle,

I secured the Camp Trophy by leaning it slightly back against the passenger seat so it would not move or tip over in transport. Due to the weight of this twenty-six inch trophy and the angle of the trophy, one of the statuettes came apart where I had welded the legs together. My heart sank. What was I going to do? After three months of meticulous work, I took the trophy back inside my home and began the process all over again for the one statuette. I removed it from the base, cleaned off the existing weld, reapplied the new bonding agent, secured the statuette in a vise using odds and ends from the family room, buffed off the excess weld, and after thirty-six hours, applied the antiquing solution. This time I had signs all over the house urging my family and friends not to slam any doors and to walk gently throughout the house. I didn't want to jar any of the five statuettes, risk another breakage, and have to start all over yet again.

Finally, the day arrived for my second attempt at transporting the Walter Camp Memorial Trophy to its original home, The University of Iowa Athletics Hall of Fame and Museum. This time I called Dale Arens, Director of the Hall of Fame and Museum, to assist me. When he arrived, I sat in the front passenger seat holding the trophy firmly in my lap. We thought about a police escort since this was truly a unique part of Hawkeye history, but we realized maybe that was going a little too far.

⌣

Nile Kinnick's legacy continues to live on year after year. Both the sixteen foot bronze statue of Nile Kinnick on the south side of Kinnick Stadium and the bronze relief artwork recessed in the brick walls of the concourse honor Nile and the 1939 Ironmen. Created by sculptor Larry Nowland, the artwork welcomes players and fans to every home football game. When the head coach and the players depart from their buses and enter the arena, they touch Nile's football helmet at the base of the statue before the team journeys into their locker room. This tradition is enjoyed by Hawkeye fans, and, it seems, his story brings in a new generation of fans every year who pay tribute to a truly outstanding man of honor, sacrifice, and proven performance; a man epitomizing a story of grit, fortitude, determination and perseverance.

Derald W. Stump, author of the book, *Kinnick...The Man and the Legend*, expressed this thought succinctly about Nile's legacy, "He left a legacy of priceless performance and an example to his country."

One of Nile's good friends, Bob Hobbs, once said, "Nile may have been beaten, but he was never defeated." Hobbs added:

"His grasp of fundamentals, his evaluation of dimensions of the contest, his awareness of the important issues in the classroom or on the field was precise and accurate, not in an egotistical way, but in the rock-solid belief that what a man could do he could - and would."

Nile Kinnick was a man for all seasons, successful in everything he did. He loved his country, the state of Iowa, and his university. Nile once said in a letter to a friend visiting the campus in Iowa City,

"It is almost like home to me. I love the campus, the people, the trees, everything about it. And it is beautiful in the spring. I hope you strolled across the golf course just at twilight and felt the peace and quiet of an Iowa evening, just as I used to do."

The praises for Nile never end. A man of wonderment with a caring, sensitive, loving spirit for those around him...truly a Hawkeye hero.

The Way of Nile
The Third Quarter,
Part One

July 1

Am more convinced than ever that DESIRE is 80% of success in athletics, probably in anything.

July 2

How people's personalities do differ. What is pleasure & quite natural to one man would be offensive & out of place in another—and it shows rare good judgment to recognize this fact.

July 3

Having enjoyed an unusual degree of publicity and popularity at one time I can see how an athlete has some difficulty in making the adjustment when his career is over. People even speak to you in a different tone. That deference once accorded is no longer observed. All that is as it should be, but nonetheless, it is a change, nay, even a letdown. Happily, I didn't have to make a real abrupt adjustment. The curtain has come down rather slowly—the eclipse wasn't immediate or total.

July 4

Independence Day—current events bring its glory into sharp relief. Allied victory in this war will mark an important milestone in world independence from tyranny.

July 5

The inequities in human relationships are many but the lot of the Negro is one of the worst. Here in the South this fact is tragically evident.

July 6

How pitiful, that in our concern for the culture of the next generation we neglect the pressing problems of our own day.

July 7

We supposedly are fighting this war to obliterate the malignant idea of racial supremacy and master-slave relationships.

July 8

(Nile wrote this in his journal on this date, a day before his July 9th birthday) My birthday—24 years on the mortal coil—happy, strenuous, endeavoring years—and what of the future? Can't view it with pessimism despite the circumstances.

July 9

The desire for certainty—unachievable in human experience—frets so many people, wears them out, robs them of happiness and peace.

July 10

(A portion of a letter that Nile wrote to his family before the 1939 football season) For three years, nay fifteen years, I have been preparing for this last year of football. The season just past has removed much of the tension that might have attended this last effort. I feel confident and free from the pressure of "absolutely necessary success" and falsely accepted responsibility. I anticipate becoming the roughest, toughest, all-around back yet to hit the conference.

July 11

What a career Churchill has had. I have had few heroes in my short life experience, but he definitely commands my admiration & respect. He has been a man of action and of resolution. He has spoken and acted in accordance with a long-run principle. He has not kowtowed to tyranny nor sacrificed fundamental truths to expediency. He does not yield! He epitomizes the staying power of the British. And what a speaker! Every word he utters makes my spine tingle.

July 12

Is there a difference between modesty and humility? May not the former be an intellectual quality and the latter a spiritual?

July 13

College exposes a man to courses in a great many fields, it opens up new vistas & possibilities but it is the continuous reading & study a man does after he graduates that determine whether he will be educated or not.

July 14

I must admit that there is nothing I enjoy more than the companionship of a beautiful woman who also possesses breeding, grace, charm and wit. There have been a few such women in my life but not enough.

July 15

…enjoy reading Tomlinson again and that scornful line—"There's sore decline in Adam's line if this be spawn of earth." Also, "The race is run by one and one, never two and two—the sin you do by two and two must be paid by one." How well I remember Prof. (Paul) Sayre quoting those lines in class one day.

July 16

…checked out a volume of Kipling's poems…He understood the thoughts and experiences of servicemen perfectly…

July 17

…in my mind, Russia is a better country in which to live than Germany. The former deplores the methods it feels it must use to gain its end, while the latter holds the bestiality, race prejudice, war, and all the indignities which it bred in the minds of its people is aim & end of the Germanic way of life.

July 18

Stayed up late last night & read through Steinbeck's short novel *The Moon is Down*. Enjoyed it very much—it is pleasantly written and presents a theme that stirs the soul of man, to wit, a free people cannot be permanently conquered.

July 19

Just as Germany failed to take England in the fall of 1940 so I believe Japan will fail to take Australia or India. And when she has been definitely halted—then will the tide turn, and the Allies will get under way.

July 20

What is so rare as a really good competitor who is unselfish.

July 21

I am experiencing a great degree of anonymity here than at any time for the past three years, perhaps longer. It is not unpleasant. In fact, in many ways it is downright enjoyable—less pressure, less responsibility, less expected of me.

July 22

Just about got a rib punched in at the supper table tonight. I ate beside a maniac. His elbows stuck out at right angles all the time he was in action—which was every minute. After awhile, with all the sarcasm I could command I said, "Pardon me, bud, but don't let me crowd you." He didn't slow down or look. He ate as if it was the last meal he expected to get on earth.

July 23

As a follow-up on the comment I made...that athletes were of much value, I want to say this. It provides a wonderful opportunity for initiating acquaintance.

July 24

Avoid the complex & fancy in thought, speech and action. Put your faith in simplicity & plain common sense.

July 25

Feel kind of low today. Used to worry about getting into a field of life endeavor that would be sure & press my capabilities. Now I am wondering whether I didn't have a rather exalted idea of the extent of those capabilities. Probably won't take much to exhaust them.

July 26

The world picture continues gloomy...the Germans continue to advance in the Caucasus, *[Caucasus: mountainous region that comprises Southeastern Russia]* the Japs are showing increased activity around Australia, India threatens to begin a civil disobedience campaign if England doesn't grant them complete freedom immediately, U.S. production is in need of steel, the shipbuilding program is in a bad way, nothing looks very good except the allies slowly...gaining air superiority everywhere—and that should win the war.

July 27

Strange, yet a good thing, the way man can become accustomed to changed circumstances.

July 28

Has capitalism—as well as Christianity—been given a fair trial?

July 29

I know that the Bible is full of stories of courage and faith that would help me a great deal - but, unhappily, I'm not as conversant with them as I would like to be.

July 30

It's somewhat of a relief to feel that it isn't imperative to do my utmost every minute I'm out on the field. I never want to work as hard at athletics again as I did in the fall of 1939. It paid dividends & was a great experience—but never again.

July 31

Constant profanity is not exactly an admirable trait, and yet the conversational profanity of some men seems quite natural, not in the least offensive, and frequently very amusing. Nonetheless, were I to adopt this as part of my personality makeup it would end in dismal failure, I am sure.

August 1

A society must earn what it receives or it will disintegrate for lack of character. A gov't which ignores this demand is a deceiver and deception in gov't is the highest of crimes.

August 2

I am far from being soured on football; I enjoy it and look forward to next season (1939); but I deplore the shape it is taking, and regret that the athletes are being exploited in the interest of a misguided public opinion. This tendency is slowly but surely driving the college student-athlete, who plays for fun and recreation, out of participation and is divorcing the game from the university.

August 3

Service life and the prospect of the future kind of stifles the ambition—at least the tendency exists. One thing is certain—when this is all over I'll have a much greater appreciation for those things in civilian life which I used to take for granted.

August 4

Can the prospect of power, prestige, recognition, take the place of profit incentive?

August 5

My three hours of solo today were most enjoyable—my wingovers were good & I successfully slipped to the circle time and again. In fact, I experimented in several ways today just for the fun & practice.

August 6

(About boxer Joe Lewis) He takes them all on anywhere, any time. They can talk all they want about the old timers, about the lack of good opposition, but I still think he is one of the best fighters who ever drew on a glove. But even more to his credit is the way he has conducted himself as champion. He has remained quiet and courteous through-out it all—no braggadocio, no alibis. Truly he has been a credit to the fighting games and to a downtrodden race. Good for him!

August 7

I reiterate that the fare is good but you don't want to enter the mess hall without warming up. You don't have a chance if you do. It's every man for himself & devil take the hind-most which is an empty platter.

August 8

Can't help making the observation that the college athletes that I know of at this base are the ones who do the least bitching at work detail to be done and who most energeti-cally attempt what is required of them.

August 9

There seem to be several popular songs right now that I like a lot—*Elmer's Tune, Chattanooga Choo Choo, Blues in the Night, Moonlight Cocktail, White Cliffs of Dover, This Love of Mine.* Can even recognize them without much trouble which is pretty good for me. Still like to listen to cowboy & hill-billy songs, though.

August 10

There [are] a good many things I don't like about military life—and there undoubtedly will be more. But, none the less, the education and experience gained in military service is invaluable, I am sure. I believe I would like to have my boys attend West Point or Annapolis after a couple of years of L.A. school, if they so desired.

August 11

More than once in the past few months, speeches that I have made have come to mind. It is strange that what I considered then as a pretty good talk now seems naïve, unimpressive, possessing little merit. Sometimes I momentarily feel embarrassed—I wonder what others thought—would it all have been better unsaid?

August 12

(About boxer Joe Lewis) ...knocked out Abe Simon in the sixth tonight. The proceeds were to go for a service benefit fund. Joe was "fighting for nothing but my country" as he put it. He is one of my favorite athletes, and a truly great champion in my mind.

August 13

Got a faint idea of what a dive bomber's perspective is by nosing my plane straight down and holding it there for awhile before pulling out. It is great fun, the trees come hurtling up at you, the wind screeches by; all this at 120 knots.

August 14

My flirtation with mediocrity in flying the past month or so has settled into something more permanent. Am not discouraged with my progress, but it isn't quite as sharp as it might be. However, it may be just as well to proceed at this gait. Certainly, it is easier on the nerves and energy.

August 15

Our social & economic problems are fundamentally moral. Their ultimate solution depends on the home, school & church.

Photographs
Military

Ensign Nile C. Kinnick, Jr. in US Navy uniform. (1943)

Kinnick in flight suit exiting from his Grumman F4F-4 Wildcat. (1943) Foster Hailey, writer for *The New York Times* said: "The Wildcat, it is no exaggeration to say, did more than any single instrument of war to save the day for the US in the Pacific."

Nile about to get drenched at one of the elimination aviation bases. Kinnick started out in Kansas City, Kansas, then went to the Pensacola, Florida, "E" Base. He was part of Flight Class 2B-42-P(C) and sworn in as a cadet. (February, 1942)

Kinnick in his US Naval Air Corps Reserve uniform.

Nile Kinnick (1st row, lower left) with fellow students who are being taught to be Naval Officers as well as aviators.

Kinnick studying to become an ensign and a fighter pilot. (April 1, 1942)

Nile standing next to his carrier-based aircraft.

The Way of Nile

The Third Quarter,

Part Two

August 16

(A letter to his family after the 1938 Purdue game) Dear Family: Today Iowa played a ball game—a REAL ball game. We fought hard, played hard for sixty minutes and had a whee of a time. We tackled hard, blocked hard and did everything but win. Our line whipped their line…the same line that held Minnesota for four downs on the one-foot line and three or four times held Minnesota inside the ten-yard line, the same line that tied Fordham. Before the game, Jimmy Fay of Emmentsburg gave us a little talk, and he hit the nail on the head. He voiced just the sentiments I've been trying to get across since I came down here. He said, 'This university will be here for years to come. There will be alumni and newspapers, but you guys don't owe them—the state, the university, the alumni, the student body—One Damn Thing! You are not obligated in any way to them; you have no responsibility apart from doing your best…for the fun of it…go out and play the game that you know you are capable of playing.' Out of these trying times, Iowa is going to emerge on a sound foundation.

August 17

A man must never cease growing, developing, looking ahead. Be alert, be vigorous, cultivate the mind & memory continually—laugh a lot.

August 18

Order vs liberty—vigor, efficiency, incentive of private enterprise & ownership vs organizational power of gov't & its assurance of greater social & economic equality & justice—how to reconcile them? Importance of the middle class in the progress of society? How to make nationalism serve the cause of internat'l cooperation.

August 19

...I can't help noting the difference in the pictures I see of Stalin & Hitler. The former has a kindly, cheerful looking face, he cannot be all bad, I'm sure. But Hitler is always the epitome of fanatical hatred, & prejudice. He looks like a maniac. I end this by stating my admiration for the courage & staying power of the Russian armies. I hope they have what it takes come spring.

August 20

Abrupt change of institutional habits is no easier than similar change in pers. [*personal*] habits.

August 21

Profit is a legitimate incentive but it must go hand in hand with the grander aim maximum production at low costs.

August 22

(About American democracy) Am. Demo. was founded & can only succeed on a thoroughly moral basis—common respect for innate dignity of man necessary—a profound sense of justice for all—closely knit family life & sound, efficient local self-gov't required.

August 23

(Nile's hyperbole) Sunset in the harbor—a suffusion of gold & scarlet lingering over the bank of purple clouds in the west—freighters at anchor—blinking semaphore signals, silent but articulate—ferry boat—strange, clamoring cry (squeak) of the sea gulls—quiet, peaceful.

August 24

Are the old virtues of thrift, hard work, initiative no longer important?

August 25

Even the broad minded members of the privileged class are prone to worship stability—need to be shaken from the apathy, shamed from their apprehension of change.

August 26

The sound, honest way to aid underprivileged individuals & nations is to help them help themselves, enable them to become strong and productive. Paternalism is but a stop gap and a contemptible one at that.

August 27

Carrier duty would be exciting, adventurous, full of action, requiring the utmost in skill and daring. All of which suddenly recalls to me a statement of Richard Hillary's in his fine book, *Falling Through Space*—"in war one can swiftly develop all one's faculties to a degree it would take a half a lifetime to achieve."

August 28

(*About going to war*) What the future will hold no man can say. Whether I shall get back to law school I don't know. It could very possibly be that something will open up through this experience that will be more to my liking than anything I have yet thought of. In any event I am going with both fists swinging expecting to make the best of whatever comes up.

August 29

Is this war a people's revolution or a struggle for survival or both?

August 30

Continually strive for improvement in writing and speaking, enlarge your vocabulary, discipline your thinking processes, develop your memory powers, try for at least twos in your schoolwork, and without turning thought in on the physique develop your muscles until you are as strong as an ox.

August 31

Monopolies formed for the purpose of restricting production & thus controlling the price structure is a crime against
society and the free enterprise system.

September 1

The Constitution is a magnificent instrument but it is not a
dispensation from on high. We must not be afraid to let it
grow & change, nor to fear a liberal interpretation in the interest of social gain & justice. However, let our aim & means
be frank and honest. The danger lies in deception & crafty
circumvention.

September 2

Under the influence of liquor men can justify action which
they would deplore when sober.

September 3

If the general standard of living is increased thru gov't
ownership & control why be alarmed at the bureaucracy &
inefficiency, debt increase, etc., or do they bring disaster in
the long run?

September 4

How can any political candidate be really free & independent in thought & policy when he is dependent on wealthy
backers for campaign funds? Is there any practical remedy
for this seemingly inescapable situation.

September 5

If we are to have an economy of abundance our productive forces must operate at capacity, but a man must always be made to earn what he receives, & those who produce more must receive more; also ingenuity & merit must be rewarded. A society which does not recognize this fundamental fact must surely disintegrate.

September 6

What is wrong with running a gov't on a fear & favor basis as the New Deal is prone to do—much needed legislation has been passed hasn't it?

September 7

Without self-respect there can be no character.

September 8

We saw Sally Rand put on her bubble & fan dance at the Towers Theatre tonight. Can't recommend it very highly. Doesn't begin to compare with Gypsy Rose Lee's performance at the Worlds Fair in New York. The latter's act bordered on artistic it was so cleverly done. This is heresy coming from a moral man, but nonetheless, true.

September 9

(A portion of a letter written to his brother Ben when he was in flight training) Don't try to get too fancy in your prayer. There will be times when you know the truth so absolutely that it doesn't even permit of word articulation in your thought...

because God is all-in-all...When you understand a problem that way, you are on the beam. If the results seem a little slow just be patient, hang on. Love more, be more grateful.

September 10

Nothing worries and wearies a man so much as trying to achieve absolute certainty in human affairs.

September 11

...agriculture; the farmer and his soil, his house, his pigs, chickens, cattle, etc.; the farmer with manure on his boots, nails in his pockets, rips in his shirt, tobacco on his breath, but by the God Almighty an honest, weatherbeaten, straightforward, courageous face.

September 12

Heretofore, American political parties have automatically taken diametrically opposite views and the country has managed to progress regardless. This can no longer be true. In this respect W. Willke has shown himself a man of much stature & character.

September 13

Don't confuse resignation with patience.

September 14

Prices cannot be successfully controlled by legislative fiat, nor even by tyranny. It can only be done by competition of the buyer & seller in the free mkt.

September 15

Monopolies can be broken by anti-trust suits or subjected to the competition of a gov't owned business in the same field.

September 16

If we expect to avoid disastrous repercussions in our economy after the war we must be as tough on the home front as we are on the fighting front.

September 17

What gov't control may sometimes be necessary (in wartime, monopolistic inequities) can best be exercised by influence in the fundamental fields of demand & supply. For example, purchasing power can be curtailed through taxation & enforced savings. Supply can be regulated through rationing or subsidies.

September 18

The time to levy heavy taxes to meet a mounting war debt is during the war itself when the people are in the spirit to accept the sacrifice & when they are necessary anyhow as an anti-inflation measure. The New Deal is doing this country a disservice in this respect.

September 19

(About the Bible) It is practical teaching & its application is sorely needed in the world today.

September 20

The conditions under which these coal miners live—and the Negroes in the South—is a shameful blot on our democratic ideals and the potential standard of living in this country.

September 21

"From each according to his ability, to each according to his work"—this may point a workable mean between the extremes of capitalism & Communism.

September 22

It is true that the common people will suffer more from such measures than the wealthy, but it will be a minor sacrifice compared to what they will have to endure if we are snowed under by a run-away inflation.

September 23

I am learning once again to read leisurely, with patience and thoughtfulness.

September 24

The Bible is a great and good book well deserving the reverence & respect it has commanded up through the ages. It is fine literature, interesting history, and full of the wisdom and experiences of a people who loved God.

September 25

(About the Bible) ... best of all a spiritual understanding of its inspired word will bring the same comfort and healing that it did in the early days of Christianity.

September 26

Now there is the matter of the noisy, prolonged laughter at movies & stage plays which make it impossible to hear the succeeding remarks and repartee. Truly the loud laugh & the vacant mind travel hand in hand.

September 27

Parents should guide & discipline their children so that they will learn their lessons of life by minor experiences of grief & mistake. Too much warning, restrictions & prohibitions bring rebellion sooner or later with all its sad consequences.

September 28

Give way easily in trivialities but stand without yielding in matters of principle.

September 29

(After visiting family and friends in Iowa) In your company all tension and worldly care disappeared; love and affection and all that is good shone bright...I hope you realize how proud I am of the spirit and sacrifice you are showing in the face of this war. You have raised us boys under the solemn edict that there shall never be any compromise with evil, that principle must always be supported regardless of the

odds, that the way is through, not around. And now you are meeting the supreme test with consummate courage. You are sending Ben and me off to battle with no display of the heroic or the dramatic, and in the quiet faith that God protects those who do their moral duty. I cannot begin to tell you how proud and happy I am. In truth you are noble people.

September 30

It is not enough for the privileged to treat the less fortunate, or the whites to treat colored people, with kindly tolerance and indulgent paternalism.

Dedication

Chapter Four

B eing a longtime Hawkeye fan, as well as supporting and graduating from The University of Iowa, it has always been my intent to someday "give back" to this outstanding institution for all that I've received. I've always felt deeply connected to Iowa City and love and respect The University of Iowa for the educational program I was part of in order to become a teacher. Researching, authoring, and publishing a book of inspirational quotes and insights about Nile Kinnick's life is my contribution and my way of saying thank you. Researching about Nile's athleticism, intelligence, and exemplary moral character only added to my enthusiasm for this book and continually empowered me to write and complete my "labor of love" task over a ten-year period.

When did my "give back" attitude begin? Being born in Iowa City, my Hawkeye fandom began as an eight-year-old exploring, with friends, the Pentacrest—the four buildings surrounding the Old Capitol—on The University of Iowa campus. Delivering the *Daily Iowan* newspaper as an elementary and junior high student enabled me to read about the Hawks. Sneaking into Iowa Hawkeye football and basketball games solidified my status as a fan. And selling "soda pop" in Iowa Stadium opened my eyes to the vastness of the football arena. When employed as a high school student for The University's mowing crew during the summer, I became even more familiar with the Field House and The University Hospital. As a result, I developed a deeper understanding of where I lived.

As a ten-year-old fifth grader at Herbert Hoover Elementary School in Iowa City, one of my most memorable adventures growing up was riding and sleeping on a train, the California Zepher. Heading west through the mountains, our destination was Pasedena, California. When my family and I arrived in California, little did I know that part of this vacation would be attending the 1957 Rose Bowl football game with my dad and uncle. What an adventure and thrill it was seeing the Hawks beat Oregon State College surrounded by 100,000 people and taking pictures with my Brownie camera that I still have over sixty years later! Some people have said that I was "born a Hawkeye." I may actually bleed, as the saying goes, "black and gold."

As a volunteer at the Iowa Athletics HOF since 2002, my Hawkeye passion and enthusiasm to "give back" to The University has led me to many enjoyable tasks. When meeting and greeting groups visiting the building, I enjoy sharing what I know about the athletes inducted into the HOF. As an ambassador, I lead students and adult groups on tours throughout the museum talking about the history of Iowa athletics and the Hawkeye memorabilia displayed in the showcases. Over the years, I've had the thrilling opportunity to host former student-athletes being inducted into the HOF and/or returning to Iowa City for special reunions and anniversaries.

In 2003, as an ambassador, I volunteered to design an exhibit for the Iowa State Fair promoting the HOF. Another task was installing the "Herkys on Parade" in the Iowa City area in 2004 with Iowa football legend Chad Greenway. I have researched and designed several displays for the HOF. In addition, it was an honor to assist Jim Heims, a great Hawkeye fan and supporter, with the installation of Nile Kinnick's All-American plaque on the exterior wall of Kinnick Stadium. In 2006, I found great excitement and pleasure being asked to create and install three levels of Hawkeye memorabilia in the glass cases when the Paul W. Brechler Press Box at Kinnick Stadium was rebuilt.

A highlight for me was telling Nile's story at the HOF with George "Red" Frye, Kinnick's teammate; Bob Brooks, a broadcaster of the 1939 Ironmen team; and Charlie Smith, a classmate of Nile's. All of us were interviewed separately and when the editing was done, Nile's student-athlete and military careers were broadcast on a television special entitled *From Ballfields to Battlefields*. Little did I know the production, by College Sports Television, would be hosted by Senator John McCain of Arizona and narrated by Charlie Gibson, anchor of ABC News at that time.

Another pleasurable task in my effort to "give back" to The University of Iowa was to write a curriculum guide to assist ambassadors serving at the HOF. The guide was called *The Hawkeye Hunt*, a hands-on activity for student groups visiting and exploring every floor of the historic museum. This year-long writing project was designed to give current, curious, and future Hawkeye fans a memorable, pleasant, and educational experience at the HOF. During tours there is always an opportunity for ambassadors to share stories with the young fans and answer questions about the Hawks.

For years *The Hawkeye Hunt* helped youngsters appreciate Iowa's athletic history and how the Iowa men and women student-athletes, coaches, and athletic directors' contributions made Iowa's athletics programs so impressive. Seeing historic memorabilia and reading information from plaques about men and women's sports teams set the tone for nurturing enthusiastic fans with a "Go Hawks!" attitude.

Finally, one of my favorite reasons for being a volunteer ambassador at the HOF is that it gives me the opportunity to view the Nile Kinnick exhibit. The display was done so well that it provided me more information about Nile. Seeing his trophies, letters, and other memorabilia showcased and reading and studying about him gave me the push to do something I thought was unimaginable: to compile and write the contents of this book.

It took many years, "on and off," to finally complete this project, but I was persistent. From the very beginning of my research, I was hoping that someday this book would be published. Never did I expect it to be in print on the anniversary of Kinnick's hundredth birthday!

Dozens of journalists, military personnel, authors, and many other individuals have made so many respectful comments about Kinnick's capabilities over the years. Dr. Virgil M. Hancher, president of The State University of Iowa for twenty-five years, once commented about the Kinnick scholarships, saying:

"No more appropriate memorial could be created at the University than the establishment of the Nile Kinnick scholarships. The Nile Kinnick Memorial Scholarship Fund will serve to perpetuate the traditions of leadership, attainment and loyalty which reached inspired heights during Nile's days on the campus. The scholarships offer outstanding students ample means to enable them to devote their entire time to their studies and activities.

Mr. and Mrs. Kinnick, Nile's father and mother, have expressed our thought so appropriately that we wish to quote what they said, 'We feel certain that Nile would take much satisfaction in knowing that through the scholarships he will be extending a helping hand to future students of similar aspirations.'"

Kinnick's academic achievements were just as impressive as his athletic awards and honors. The University selected him as a Phi Beta Kappa scholar, the oldest and most prestigious honor society in the United States. He was elected student body president, gave the commencement speech, and had a 3.4 GPA with a degree from the College of Commerce. His first year in law school, he was third in his class. Being able to balance his academics and his performance on the football field was awe-inspiring to me.

George Trevor, a journalist from the East Coast at the time Nile won the Heisman Trophy, brilliantly expressed that the:

"square cut of Kinnick's jaw, the bulldog set of his mouth, and the look of eagles in his brown eyes, reveal the grim determination and fixity of purpose... Character is stamped

*in every line of Kinnick's alert forthright face. Intelligence
glows from his illuminous eyes."*

Bill Cunningham, a *Boston Globe* writer during that time, said
that "the country is 'okeh' as long as it produces Nile Kinnicks. The
football part is incidental."

Kinnick was a homegrown Adel, Iowa, legend, sometimes
referred to as the "Cornbelt Comet." After the second game of
the 1939 season, Tait Cummins, a journalist for the *Cedar Rapids
Gazette*, said this about Nile:

> *"A new gridiron star blazed across the Big Ten horizon here
> Saturday, a spectacular comet with brilliant touchdown
> tails which cleared away the shadows of despair which
> have hovered over Iowa's big stadium for the last six years,
> and which completely eclipsed Indiana's lesser constellation
> in a 32-29 game never equaled in Hawkeye history."*

My goal with this book was to tell a "story within a story," that
is, to share Nile's thoughts and feelings through his quotes and
how they intertwined with my personal stories. His quotes are truly
mini-stories that relate to my fascination about, admiration for,
and inspiration from Nile Clarke Kinnick, Jr.

The Way of Nile
The Fourth Quarter,
Part One

October 1

A position of leadership & responsibility should mean more work, more sacrifice, not privilege & repose.

October 2

Social & economic & racial inequities cannot be solved in a moment, & in some respects it is best that we make haste slowly, but this truth is basic and is the starting point & foundation on which to build.

October 3

(Nile's hyperbole) Flew up among the clouds today—tall, voluminous cumulus clouds—they were like snow covered mountains, range after range of them. I felt like an Alpine adventurer climbing up the canyons, winding my way between their peaks—a billowy fastness, a celestial citadel.

October 4

No man, or group of men, is wise enough to rule a country in happiness & prosperity. It takes the wisdom & perspective born of the crucible of free debate & discussion of a demo. (*democratic*) people.

October 5

(*During flight training*) It is against my nature & inclination to indict a service with such a fine tradition as the U.S. Navy. But, by golly, I'm getting pretty disgusted with the red tape, inefficiency, and disorganization around this base. I am quite aware that it is a difficult situation, that the facilities are overcrowded, and that several of the officers are products of 90 day training and therefore aren't "up" on everything they should be. However, nobody around here seems to know what the hell is going on. I have never seen so many orders & counter-mands in my life.

October 6

A gov't must do more than establish order, guarantee political liberty, and insure equal justice under law. It must stand ready to remedy abuses in the economic system, to stimulate the economy of abundance. However, in doing these things a good gov't will help the people to help themselves, never promoting the philosophy that the gov't owes its people a living.

October 7

Initiative—timely action based on sound thinking & willingness to assume the responsibility.

October 8

All people of whatever creed, nationality, or color must be accorded equal dignity and human worth. Both Christianity & true democracy demand this fundamental acknowledgment.

October 9

(During the course of the 1938 football season) I wish so fervently that we could get going for the coaches' sake—they are as fine a bunch as ever lived. The papers and wolves are after them hot and heavy—the rats.

October 10

(Before the upcoming 1939 football season) ...with the coming of spring just as the crops and gardens are budding upward so are my hopes for next year. I am looking forward to a happy, restful, companionable summer at home. What a joyous, fruitful time we should all have.

October 11

Desire for approval of associates deters the conservative, respectable people from advocating reform.

October 12

Moonbeams were dancing on the water tonight in ever changing forms—a kaleidoscope of geometric pattern— without refocusing my eyes the shapes seem to grow to become permanent as if they were traced on the bottom of a pool of water about 6' deep.

October 13

Both our Const. (*Constitution*) & our slogans have their worth and meaning, but we should not worship them superstitiously or permit them as moral argument for the suppression of the underprivileged.

October 14

(*About military marching*) He who from a normal angle of observation appeared effeminate and prissy when his walking movement was studied from the rear; he who looked relaxed and at ease from the front looked taut and strained from behind; and he who looked firm and strong was apt to appear weak and dissipated to the man walking directly behind him. Rather a bourgeoisie observation, but interesting, don't you think?

October 15

A demo. gov't whose people will not permit it to arm & act against foreign & domestic enemy—both military & econ.—is not fit to survive.

October 16

The war picture grows more grim. Valiant is the stand being made in Java, but courage is not going to be enough it appears. Where is the Japanese advance going to be checked—Australia, India? Certainly these two places are next in order for attack. All this talk in recent years of Hitler's plan to march around the oceans & join hands with Japan was not just idle speculation. Undoubtedly, there will be an all out bid in the spring by the Axis powers to join forces through India and that general area. The year 1942 will be critical—we must not falter or fail. How I would like to be in on the action by next fall!

October 17

Failure to honestly & courageously reconcile your ideals & present needs brings much distress, moral confusion.

October 18

By & large people prefer "financing" to taxation.

October 19

Always fake before you strike.

October 20

Such institutions as the church & family cannot very well sanction the easy compromise of principle and ideals because the frailties of human nature would soon run rampant and obscure the beacon which has pointed our progress.

October 21

As the gov't continues to play an even greater part in our economy & social life it is imperative that we develop a good, sound, honest, efficient system of administrators.

October 22

It is a sad mistake to try to be the head man in everything you attempt. The axiom "if its (*it's*) worth doing at all, its (*it's*) worth doing well" has its limitations. Stay on the ball most of the time, but learn to coast between moments of all-out effort.

October 23

Good conversation is more rare than good food.

October 24

The mind which demands "one or the other," "all or nothing" is the mind which can never successfully reconcile idealism with the practical need.

October 25

(*During the 1939 fall football season*) Thus far in my college career I have tasted the glory of success and the ignominy of pretty near failure—the top and the bottom. And I have now stood out against personal thought, resentment and *materia medica*, stood on what I know to be the true basis of all…I have had the courage of my convictions in those things which needed such a decision. It has not been a lot of fun nor has it been a displeasure, but certainly this fall has not been without its fruits—unseen though they may be. I trust that such experiences will enable me to stand firm under even more troubling circumstances.

October 26

Do the best that you can & the best that you know and fear not. That goes for prayer as well as other endeavors.

October 27

The Consti. (*Constitutional*) fathers were wise but also humble—I don't believe they thought they had formulated an infallible & unchanging law. It isn't a divine dispensation.

October 28

When writing or speaking don't attempt to be too precise and detailed. Leave something to the intelligence and imagination of your listeners.

October 29

Conforming or reconciling everyday action & thought to the demands of religious teaching is a potent stimulus to the active & conscientious mind.

October 30

Men are no stronger or braver than the women behind them.

October 31

If you really want to win, never give a sucker a break. Press advantage to the limit.

November 1

Christian Science, Yankee pragmatism, laughter are the tools with which I fashion my life.

November 2

Is profit an essential element of efficiency? Is he who works without a profit incentive inevitably bureaucratic? How about a professor, minister, scientist?

November 3

Gov't by force cannot last, it is too exhausting. An enduring gov't must be based on the faiths & loyalties of a people.

November 4

Why haven't I learned to shoot at least fairly well in the past 10 or 12 years I'll never know. Of all things a man needs to be good at in war, it is shooting. I must remedy this deficiency—and soon.

November 5

Given a social need plus a respectable symbol, and the means, whatever they are, will be readily countenanced.

November 6

No one particular system of gov't can solve our econ. (*economic*) & social difficulties.

November 7

Realize that every close call with danger is proof of God's care and that the demands of a tough assignment are a challenge to your worth and courage. This kind of thinking knows no fear.

November 8

Political gov't is a dramatic spectacle.

November 9

Supreme Court in their learned and august opinions are actually deciding political issues—that is, there is a limit to the judicial function.

November 10

The reconciliation of practical needs and our aspiration must be made by the individual in good conscience and without fear.

November 11

Be genuine, pleasant, tolerant—avoid pretense.

November 12

Learn to sleep soundly and efficiently regardless of circumstances if you would be a man of stamina.

November 13

We are too often prone to judge corp. (*corporations*) entirely by their successes & our gov't by its failures.

November 14

A good sense of order is a fine thing, but in certain circumstances be willing to settle for something a little short of the ideal or you will be unceasingly annoyed. The imp. (*important*) thing is to keep your thought well ordered—be able to see order in seeming chaos.

November 15

Social philosophies have significance only in relation to the conflicts out of which they arise & the institutions which they support.

Photographs
Legacy

Formal portrait of Nile. Nile's father wrote on his son's celebrity status after the 1939 season: "How the grandfathers would burst with pride if they could be here to witness the glory ... no doubt you realize how much of your success has its roots in those two grand old men."

Nile's hometown of Adel, Iowa, has a plaque in the park honoring both Kinnick and Bob Feller. Feller was a Hall of Fame baseball player. This park was the former football field where Kinnick played as a child.

Dallas County, includes Adel, Iowa, Kinnick's hometown.
The Dallas County News **honored both Nile's life and death.**

Nile in his Iowa letter jacket.

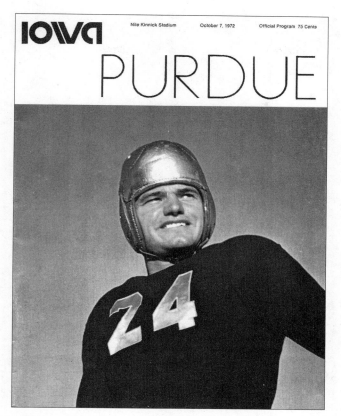

IOWA   Nile Kinnick Stadium   October 7, 1972   Official Program 75 Cents

PURDUE

Nile is featured on the cover of the 1972 football program, the year Iowa Stadium was renamed Kinnick Stadium.

A collage featuring Nile at The University of Iowa Athletics Hall of Fame and Museum.

Another exhibit featuring Nile at the Hall of Fame. Gerald Ankeny, a teammate of Nile Kinnick recalled: "Nile had a tremendous vibrancy along with a tremendous devotion to his faith and an unusual maturity for his age."

Nile Kinnick's football jersey displayed at the Hall of Fame. His number 24 is only one of two numbers to be retired.

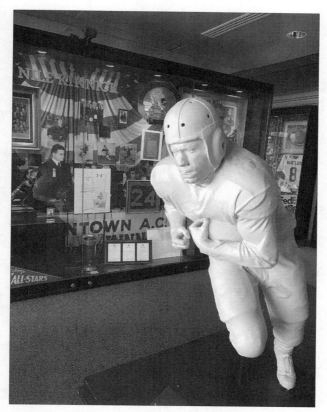

Statue of Nile Kinnick on display at the Hall of Fame.

Nile, Sr., (left) father of Kinnick, is shown with Chalmers "Bump" Elliott, athletic director at The University of Iowa. They are participating in the renaming of Iowa Stadium to Kinnick Stadium. (1972)

Sculptor Larry Nowlan working on a ten-foot by twenty-foot bronze relief honoring the "Ironmen," many of whom played all sixty minutes in the Notre Dame vs. Iowa football game.

Nolan's completed relief is shown in the south concourse of Kinnick Stadium. Featured is Nile Kinnick scoring a touchdown in the 1939 game against Notre Dame.

A bobble head of Nile Kinnick on display at the Hall of Fame. On October 23, 1943, not long after Nile's passing, well-known Iowa journalist Jim Zabel wrote: "I don't know whether the administration has made any plans to name Iowa Stadium after Nile Kinnick yet, but I hope the powers-that-be take a definite action soon ... Campus opinion is solidly behind the idea."

The unveiling of the sixteen-foot Nile Kinnick statue in 2006 at Kinnick Stadium before the preseason game against Montana. The sculpture was created by Larry Nowlan.

Nile's bronzed helmet is at the base of his statue at Kinnick Stadium. A tradition by Iowa football players honoring Nile is touching his helmet before entering the locker room.

A portion of Nile's student-athlete statue at Kinnick Stadium. Nile is wearing his letter jacket with his football jersey slung over his shoulder. A notebook and textbook are carried in his right hand.

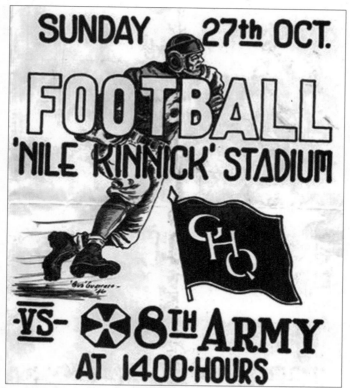

Program cover of football game between CHQ and 8th Army at Nile Kinnick Stadium in Japan in circa 1946

Nile C. Kinnick High School is a Department of Defense Educational Activity Naval School (DoDEA) currently located in US Fleet Activities Yokosuka, Japan. It was originally located in Yokohama, Japan, and called Yo-Hi. In 1959 the school went from an Army school to a Naval school and was renamed Kinnick High School.

Program cover of the 1949 New Year's Day Rice Bowl game played at Nile Kinnick Stadium in Tokyo, Japan, between the Army and Air Force All-Stars. The stadium was renamed by the Occupation Forces in 1945 in memory of Navy Ensign Nile Kinnick.

A new drill hall dedicated and named in memory of Ensign Kinnick at the US Naval Air Station in Olathe, Kansas. (August 10, 1943)

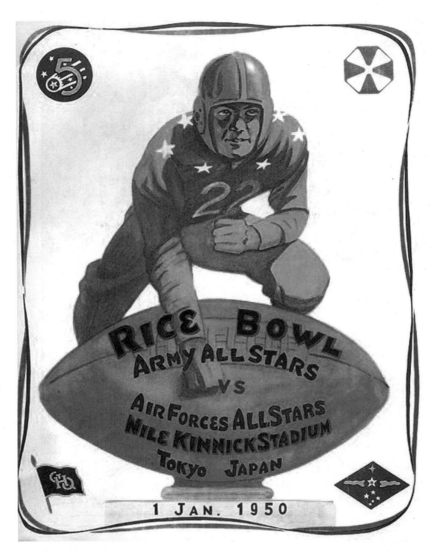

The program cover for the 1950 Rice Bowl at Nile Kinnick Stadium, formerly the Meiji Shrine Stadium. It was originally intended to be used in the 1940 Olympics as a track and field coliseum, but the Olympics were cancelled due to the outbreak of World War II.

The Way of Nile
The Fourth Quarter,
Part Two

November 16

Is this an age where organiz. [*organizations*] have replaced individ. [*individuals*] as units?

November 17

Was the exploitation of labor by the big corporations & the robbery of stock & bondholders thru bankruptcy & reorganization proceedings the result of unscrupulous action by dishonest men, or of viewing these great organizations as individuals competing in a free market without public responsibility?

November 18

May there not come a time when economic security will become as an integral part of our Bill of Rights as pers. (*personal*) security. Of course it will mean that there must be max. production and that each man shall receive according to his work & merit. Such guarantees can never spring from the logic of biology and anthropology but only from a high sense of justice, common brotherhood, and human dignity.

November 19

Good & efficient gov't in an expanding sphere requires gradual development just like private organiz. (*organizations*). It cannot be mature at the moment of birth.

November 20

Any attempt to base a philosophy of gov't on a universal truth or eternal verity (impossible in human affairs) will fail.

November 21

Those who rankle at the worship of Roosevelt's personality can destroy it only by advocating an attitude toward the function of gov't which makes that personality less imp. (*important*).

November 22

(*A letter to his family about new head coach Dr. Eddie Anderson before he arrived on campus*) …I feel quite strongly that he (Anderson) and I will get along very well. That we can forestall any clash of opinions I am quite confident. When I met him several weeks ago and spoke enthusiastically in his behalf I am sure that he was well impressed with me—as I with him. He and I will of course differ in opinions, beliefs, and convictions. However, that we must clash personally can be metaphysically obviated. He and I have good reputations; the development of which each of us attributes to diametrically opposite causes and convictions. Nevertheless, we both will be aware that our continued success may lie in cooperation and mutual effort.

November 23

(*A portion of a letter Nile wrote to his father*) I frequently think of what I shall want to do for a livelihood. Aviation will be a tremendously growing industry then, and it may be that I shall want to stay in it in some capacity or another, but right now do you know what appeals to me? I want to be a flour salesman, if there are such animals. That is, I want to hook up with some good flour company & start out as their sales representative in Iowa. My idea being that such a job would give me an opportunity to travel about the state & among the people I like—farmers & small town inhabitants. The future could have two alternatives—advancement up the ladder to the home office—or, possibly, a political campaign for senator.

November 24

The poorer element of a city will support a corrupt political machine because it gets charity without humiliation.

November 25

(*Before the 1939 football season*)…raring to go; to race up and down that field like a runaway bag of cement.

November 26

In *Look* magazine there was an interesting article on Stalin & Russia by Joseph Davies, former ambassador of the Soviet. I cannot help feeling that despite the ruthless domestic policy of the Russian gov't & its world revolutionary tendencies that something good may ultimately develop out this great experiment.

November 27

Selfish vested interests must clothe themselves with some respectable social myth, if they expect to form a powerful organization.

November 28

Is it a mistake to personify a corp. as an individual? Its "prop." (*proposition*) value is in its organization & not primarily in its tangible assets.

November 29

What part should the state gov'ts play in producing a better society & way of life? How dangerous is the growth of tolls and excise taxes on traffic between states.

November 30

A good leader in gov't must be a good organizer, also tolerant & humanitarian.

December 1

Under the banner of "laissez faire" & business competition men can justify methods which are entirely foreign to their personal nature.

December 2

Are big businessman who force their employees to work under poor conditions, pay low wages, sell their products at artificially high prices, & yet are great personal philanthropists—are they hypocrites or just observing a fundamental principle of human org. [*organization*]?

December 3

Tomorrow I report at Kansas City for elimination training in the U.S. Naval Reserve Air Corps. I am looking forward with enthusiasm to this new experience. I am fully aware that this country is on the brink of a shooting war in two oceans and that I might, in a very short while, find myself in the thick of very serious combat work. But what should be done, can be done, and the best way is always through not around.

December 4

An honest, just, humanitarian pragmatism is the answer—a realistic understanding of political dynamics.

December 5

An honest, conscientious reconciliation of conflicting ideals is absolutely necessary for practical efficient results.

December 6

As I hoped, this year is seeing a filling out of my college activities—a play here, a lecture there, a quiet bit of repose, an engaging piece of leisurely conversation, a date now and then (sometimes oftener)—all make for what I feel a man should get in his four years of college.

December 7

News of Japan's unprovoked attack on Pearl Harbor came over the radio about three o'clock p.m. About a third of us were lounging around the barracks. Everybody accepted it quite unemotionally, seemingly more interested in whether liberties would be curtailed than whether the U.S. could retaliate effectively.

December 8

(*In a letter to his brother George*) The only real joy and strength in life is found in loving your fellow man, finding yours in another's good. The keys to happiness are patience, good humor, unselfishness—and it takes a lifetime to demonstrate all this. Never let momentary feelings deter you from pressing on, or even starting anew. Just passing thought, George, served cafeteria style...look or help yourself according to your fancy.

December 9

As for my own feelings now that the US & Japan are at war I shall say this. I expected it but not quite so soon. I expected to be faced with the prospect of serious combat action when I joined up. I am ready for whatever it may be my duty to do. I feel much as I used to when the football season started and I knew Minnesota was on the schedule. That is, I realize what is coming up but probably won't get appreciably keyed up until actually moving onto the firing line.

December 10

I would add this rule for becoming a good officer. You shouldn't ask your men what you won't do yourself.

December 11

(*During World War II*) Picked up a biography of Mr. Churchill just recently written by Philip Guedalla. Read it straight through and found it extremely interesting, as I always do anything that concerns Britain's sturdy Prime Minister. He is the man in history who has completely caught my fancy and imagination. I read his every speech and writing with absorbing interest. He is a man of thought, of action, of resolution, and the man in the hour in the world's greatest crisis.

December 12

Every man whom I have admired in history has willingly and courageously served his country's armed forces in times of danger. It is not only a duty, but an honor, to follow their example as best I know how.

December 13

If I were home…I know one thing I would do for certain. I would read out loud that delightful little poem, *The Night Before Christmas* and also Dicken's *Christmas Carol*. Then I'd sit back and enjoy the traditional C'mas music, *Silent Night*,

O Little Town of Bethlehem, and *Jingle Bells*…That kind of Christmas seems rather important to me now.

December 14

The spirit & the letter are complements one of the other, as are faith & understanding, but prefer the simple to the fancy or complex if you would triumph.

December 15

Expectation of absolute certainty in human affairs through prayer results in frustration, exhaustion.

December 16

(Nile's thoughts about the upcoming 1939 football season)
Yesterday I talked with Anderson for awhile and am still more favorably impressed than the first time. He is a forceful character and seems to know his stuff…he said that he was counting on me to call signals from the left halfback post; that by next fall he expected me to know more about calling signals and different formations than any of the opposing coaches; that if all he has heard about me is true I should be the best back in the country next year. All of which sounds quite rosy, but I shan't be put off my base or guard the least bit. However, I can't deny that I was happy to hear him say this for the simple reason that I have practiced all my life to learn to run, throw and kick and haven't, as yet in college, had the opportunity to show myself a good single wing back.

December 17

(*About World War II*) If Russia continues to build her world prestige with military victories, what problem the U.S. will have with Communists in this country! Must England & the U.S. end up fighting that outfit, too? It looks like a pretty rough & rocky road ahead.

December 18

Thought and action which centres around self can only bring unhappiness, vexation.

December 19

If you cannot meet the moral demands of abstinence and continence, then for goodness sake at least be temperate, discriminating, discreet—be civilized.

December 20

How wonderful it will be when the war is won, and we are back together again. Home and family means so much to me. Hope you realize how grateful I am...Your devotion and affection have determined what I am and what I shall be. In the years to come we shall certainly share even finer enjoyments.

December 21

(*A poem Nile wrote to his brother George*)
Oh, I long for Christmas back in Iowa,
Where the landscape is white with snow,
Where the ponds and rivers freeze,

And the north wind is sure to blow.

I want to slam down on my sled,
Cut a figure eight with my skates;
Do all those things I used to do,
Before we began to play for higher stakes.

Race out of the cold in by the fire,
Soon warm before the flickering blaze,
With popcorn to eat and stories to tell.
Who doesn't yearn for those wonderful days?

Christmas without cold and snow is not the same.
It's like a picture without a frame.

December 22
Privilege without responsibility soon becomes tyranny.

December 23
For me the grievous world situation dimmed not at all the significance of Christmas Day.

December 24
(*A portion of a letter Nile wrote to his family after the loss to Michigan in 1939*) Dear family: First of all I want to thank you, father, for your fine letter received in Jackson, Michigan. It was one of the finest I have ever received from you and there have been many of them…I don't know how a son could go out and play it over; that is the ruthless part of this game sometimes…once it is over nothing can be done

about it…It breaks my heart to have sort of let him down. He really is a fine fellow and a swell coach. (*Coach Anderson*)

December 25

(*On Christmas Day, 1941*) Peace on earth, good will toward men is having a hard go these days. However, I am sure that this present world war which has engulfed the U.S. these past few weeks did not spoil the Kinnick family's enjoyment of this holy day. I think the world situation only caused us to hold it that much more dear…our whole family, individually and collectively, faces troublesome situations without any display of emotion or self-pity. I could not help noticing, however, that father was more serious than I had ever seen him before, and that mother had tears in her eyes, when I bid them good-bye.

(*To his parents on Christmas Day, 1942*) This is Christmas Day, and I must have a talk with you even though we are half a continent apart. Sitting here all alone in my room my thought constantly turns to the holiday seasons we used to enjoy in Adel…Remember how we used to go coasting morning and afternoon, and, sometimes, even after supper. And Schwartz's pond, the first body of water to freeze solid enough for skating each winter…(the Schwartz's) asking us in to get warm, feeding us popcorn and fudge, showing every concern for our comfort and happiness…

December 26

Well, the Heisman award has come to me. Be that as it may, it really is a tribute to a fine Iowa squad and a great coaching staff. I wish we might all have gone to New York to receive it together. Goodbye, 1939. There will never be another season like you.

December 27

When this war is over the colored problem is apt to be more difficult than ever. May wisdom, justice, brotherly love guide our steps to the right solution.

December 28

Can fully appreciate your attachment to Iowa. I feel the same way. The climate in the south is enervating, tends to rob you of spirit and energy. Give me the Midwest where the season's change, where summer is hot and you can see the corn grow; where winter is cold and snow beautifies the landscape; where fall and spring are the most pleasant, most happy & most joyful time of the year—and give me especially the state of Iowa where all the people are straight forward, friendly, and strictly 4.0.

December 29

(*A portion of a letter Nile wrote to his mother after winning the John P. Laffey Law Scholarship Award for first-year students*) I wish you would help me in the line of proper guidance as to the future. From this experience I feel pro ball is not the right direction, and yet I don't want to pass it by if it seems to be the ultimate consummation of my endeavors in this field. I hardly think it is, however. I have no desire to play nor hesitancy about passing up the money, though I suppose it will look awfully big in a few years.

December 30

Don't let anyone or anything or any combination of circumstances rob you of your enthusiasm for this game....of your ability to play it for fun. Coaches will sharply criticize, reporters will ridicule, and encouragement from all quarters may be lacking, but don't become a laggard or a cynic. Stick out your chin and come back for more.

December 31

The athlete learns to evaluate…to evaluate between athletics and studies, between playing for fun and playing as a business, between playing clean and playing dirty, between being conventional and being true to one's convictions. He is facing the identical conditions [that] will confront him after college…the same dimensions and circumstances. But how many football players realize this?

Epilogue

by Jim Leach

⮑

Descended from one of the earliest settler families attracted to the fertile rolling plains of central Iowa, Nile Clarke Kinnick, Jr. was born and raised in Adel, a classic county seat town, in 1918, the last year of World War I. His father, an agronomist, was a graduate of the country's first land-grant college, now known as Iowa State University. His grandfather on his mother's side, George W. Clarke, a graduate of the University of Iowa Law School, was a former Speaker of the Iowa House of Representatives and thence a two-term Progressive Era Governor of Iowa (1913-1917). Upon leaving office, Governor Clarke became dean of the Drake University Law School.

Young Nile was raised as a member of the Christian Science Church, a faith system imbued by its founder, Mary Baker Eddy, with thought-provoking moral pinions. "The sole reality of existence," Eddy wrote, is "Life in and of Spirit." Committed to his faith, Kinnick developed a Gandhi-like concern for right and wrong. It led him to emphasize self-assessment, self-effort, and selfless concern for others.

An incident illustrates his moral compass.

In the mid-1970s as a first time candidate for Congress I was handing out small campaign cards to passer-bys on Clinton Street in Iowa City opposite the Old Capitol building when a professor stopped and introduced himself. He noted, perhaps because it was a football weekend, that near where I was then standing he as a graduate student toting books from the library had once met Nile Kinnick. Immediately I asked if he remembered the conversation. The professor replied that Kinnick didn't speak to him; he spoke to the others. I inquired what he meant and he described how two inebriated young men had confronted him with a cascade of anti-Semitic aspersions. At which point, Nile Kinnick wearing his letter jacket happened upon the scene. Overhearing the taunts, he stopped and turned on the fractious duo with a rebuke the professor said he would never forget. In a low, firm voice Kinnick said that if he heard one more hateful remark he would personally thrash each of them. Cowed, the chastised walked on. Saying nothing further, Kinnick simply nodded to the offended scholar and continued his walk in the opposite direction.

The Kinnicks and the Clarkes were multi-generation neighbors of my father's family in Adel. Indeed, Kinnick's grandfather, George W. Clarke, had his law office on the second floor of the community bank my great-grandfather, S.M. Leach co-founded on the Adel town square. In one of the most stirring events in the town's history, S.M. Leach in 1895 was shot in the neck and shoulder and nearly killed by two men from a neighboring county who attempted to rob the bank. Hearing noise below, Clarke rushed down to see what caused the ruckus. One of the bank robbers stuck his Spencer repeating shot gun in his chest and pulled the trigger. Fortuitously, the gun misfired, allowing the future governor of Iowa to skip back up the stairs to fetch a firearm from his office.

The bank had just opened when the would-be robbers burst into its lobby. Leach had previously placed a small bag of money on the counter and was in the process of carrying a second larger bag from the vault to prepare for the day's business when he found shot guns pointing at him. Refusing to give up the bag that he had just retrieved, he was immediately shot. Despite being badly wounded, he threw the larger bag back into the safe and closed its door. The robbers were left with the only option of fleeing in their horse-drawn buggy with the smaller bag that contained $272.30.

A posse quickly formed and chased the culprits seven miles from town along the South Racoon River. After one of the horses pulling the buggy was shot, they took off on foot. One was soon captured hiding in the woods. The other sought refuge in a barn. Fearful that he might be lynched on the spot, the captured robber, was coerced into carrying a can of kerosene, pouring it on a stack of straw and fodder next to the barn, and setting it on fire. As a consequence his partner in crime was riddled with bullets as the smoke forced him to emerge from the burning barn. That evening a mob formed at the county jail intent on lynching the surviving robber. The sheriff stood his ground and the mob eventually disbursed after the town doctor announced that S.M. Leach and five other bystanders who had also been wounded during the robbery were expected to recover.

The next day a grim picture on the front page of the local newspaper showed a dead body strapped to a chair in front of the Adel State Bank with blood-stained bullet holes clearly evident. To underscore how post-frontier justice was upheld in Dallas County, Iowa, the picture's caption read: "This is what happens to bank robbers who come to Adel."

Decades later bank robberies became standard grist in Western movie plots. But by the turn of the 19th to the 20th Century when most counties in Iowa peaked in population, rural criminality had become a cultural aberration. County seat towns had become centers of heartland values. Nile Kinnick is thus a product of what had become a vibrant rural way of life. He grew up in a secure community under the umbrella of a warm family in a neighborhood teeming with boyhood friends. Virtually every day of the year he played ball of one kind or another. In the spring and summer he batted and caught baseballs, a sport which is a distant adaptation of cricket that in England dates back to the 16th Century; in the fall football, which is a first cousin of British rugby; and in the winter basketball, a uniquely American invention.

In May of 1929, four months before a stock market crash precipitated the Great Depression, Nile as a ten-year old sixth grader wrote my father, then a student at the University of Iowa, to thank him for a baseball he had sent as an early birthday present. In many ways the hand-written letter Nile wrote reflects as much as any of his later writings how his small town background shaped his values. Sent with a 2-cent stamp, Nile wrote:

"The ball you sent us has been a joy not to us alone but to the whole sixth grade baseball team. The sixth grade had two baseball games this week, one with the seventh grade which we beat eighteen to seven and another game with the eighth grade which we also beat twenty-four to nineteen. A good ball is just what we needed... Tuesday night we had a picnic of which something happened that will make us remember that picnic forever. The excitement that befell us was that we had some hamburger flattened out in little round pats ready to be put in the skillet which we had on

the edge of two rocks with the fire under it when somebody yelled, we turned around to find George {the family dog} being lifted out of the middle of the hamburgers by Uncle Charlie with hamburger on each foot... Yours in thanks, June" {an abbreviated family knick-name for 'Junior'}

When Nile became a teenager he joined a county-wide American Legion baseball team and became the catcher for the Hall of Fame pitcher, Bob Feller, who was from nearby Van Meter. Feller and his brother-in-law, Hal Manders, who also pitched in the Major Leagues, once visited my congressional office. I asked Feller what he remembered of Nile and he grinned and said that what he most appreciated was that "Nile could catch me." His comment was no slight compliment in that "Bullet Bob" Feller was renowned for throwing harder than any mid-Century pitcher. Indeed, Feller may have been the first Major League pitcher to be timed with cumbersome equipment, once in Cleveland, once in Washington, D.C. The speeds registered were 107 and 108 miles per hour. When queried, Feller would note that he could pitch faster, especially when he was younger, but was confident he could average these speeds for a full game. As his American Legion catcher, Nile Kinnick must have had the sorest hand in the county.

The other anecdote Feller recalled was that Nile always brought a football to the ball park with him. In "down times" on the diamond he would practice drop kicking, an art his father—a former Iowa State University quarterback—taught him. Nile approached games as a competitor but treated the nuances of sports as a craft. While drop kicking gradually became obsolete in football, it is no fluke that in Iowa's 1939 victory over Notre Dame this kicking craftsman punted for 731 yards, an Iowa single game record that eight decades later still stands.

Life has many dimensions. People, like countries, are wise to learn both from their mistakes and from what has proven over time to be effective. Experience teaches that what most uplifts people and nations are inspirational stories. For instance, there are many great American athletes. But few stories are more inspiring than that of Nile Kinnick and the Iowa team he played on—the 1939 "Ironmen". Like his team-mates, Kinnick played both offense and defense, in his case, 98% of all plays over the season. Throwing and running, he was responsible for 84% of Iowa's touchdowns. And on defense he set a long-standing team record for interceptions.

For his accomplishments and his team's success, Kinnick was awarded the Heisman Trophy, the Walter Camp Memorial Trophy, and the Maxwell Award. Uniquely, he also became the first collegiate football player to be designated Male Athlete of the Year by the Associated Press. Twelve years later Nile Kinnick was posthumously inducted into the inaugural classes of both the College Football Hall of Fame and the Iowa Sports Hall of Fame.

Even though he had scored two touchdowns and made four extra points in the 1940 College All-Star Game against the reining NFL champions, the Green Bay Packers, and even though he was offered an opportunity to play major league baseball as well as professional football, Kinnick chose to enroll in The University of Iowa Law School. A Phi Beta Kappa scholar, class president, and commencement speaker as an undergraduate, he came to rank 3rd in his law school class after his first and what proved to be only year in law school. Other duties called.

In December, 1941, two years after his Heisman Trophy acceptance speech in which he so profoundly thanked God that he was born "to the grid irons of the middle west and not to the battle fields of Europe," Nile Kinnick reported for induction into the United States Navy. Three days later the Japanese attacked Pearl Harbor.

On June 2, 1943, a Grumman F4F Wildcat on a training flight from the aircraft carrier USS Lexington developed an incapacitating oil leak in the Gulf of Paria off the coast of Venezuela. The body of its pilot, Ensign Nile Kinnick, was never recovered.

To this day the Nile Kinnick story lives on, inspiring Americans of all ages and walks of life...especially those Hawkeye fans who on Saturday afternoons in the fall walk past his statue on the way into Kinnick Stadium.

Jim Leach began a public career as a US Foreign Service Officer at the Department of State. In 1973 he returned to his home town (Davenport) and three years later was elected to Congress where he served for thirty years. Upon leaving Congress he was appointed the John L. Weinberg Visiting Professor of Public and International Affairs at the Woodrow Wilson School of Princeton University. Subsequently he was appointed a lecturer and interim Director of the Institute of Politics at the Harvard Kennedy School. President Obama then named Leach the ninth Chair of the National Endowment for the Humanities. Four years later he accepted a dual appointment as The University of Iowa Chair of Public Affairs and Visiting Professor of Law.

ACKNOWLEDGEMENTS

The Way of Nile took over ten years to research and compile the 366 memorable quotes from Nile Clarke Kinnick, Jr.'s diaries, journals, letters, and speeches. The book also includes four personal stories connecting periods of my life to Nile's wit and wisdom from his student-athlete and military service years. To have this book published was a task that could not have been accomplished alone. Without the following individuals as my mentors, this book would never have come to fruition.

I want to express my sincere gratitude to David R. Dierks, one of the vice presidents of The University of Iowa Foundation (currently renamed the U of I Center for Advancement). When I approached Dave in February of 2016, I shared with him the rough draft of my project about Kinnick and explained that I wanted to gift the royalties from this book to help fund six Nile Kinnick scholarships. Dave was on board and excited about the project and wanted to gather input from others within the Foundation. For over two years, we have been exchanging thoughts, and with his incredible support, this book has become a reality.

During this same time frame, I shared my draft with a long-time friend of mine, former US Air Force jet pilot and commander Colonel Robert A. Stein, a graduate of The University of Iowa. Bob has authored six novels, co-authored three screenplays, and a U of I Writers' Workshop student and instructor. His enthusiasm for this project and support were invaluable. During this endeavor, Stein contacted Dierks and told him about Steve Semken, a well-known publisher in North Liberty, Iowa, who might be interested in the book. Dierks contacted Semken and the rest is history.

Another person I want to thank is my publisher/editor, Steve Semken, owner of Ice Cube Press, LLC. Steve challenged me by suggesting that I write four stories connecting portions of my life to Nile Kinnick's memorable quotes. The task was daunting but well worth it. Semken's experience, professionalism, and suggestions guided me through the writing process.

Two references that helped me in this project were: *A Hero Perished. The Diary & Selected Letters of Nile Kinnick*. Baender, Paul, editor. (University of Iowa Press, 1991) and *Kinnick: The Man and the Legend*. Stump, D. W. (University of Iowa Press, 1975).

Finally, I want to thank Pam, my dear wife and best friend. Her tremendous help with editing, providing feedback, and the giving of her time were gratefully and deeply appreciated.

About the Author

Mark D. Wilson was born and raised in Iowa City, Iowa, the home of The University of Iowa Hawkeyes, and has lived there his entire life. He received his BA and MA degrees in education at The University of Iowa and went on to have a successful thirty-year elementary teaching career in the Iowa City Public School District serving disadvantaged students who were at-risk of failure in reading. He was honored by receiving Educator of the Year and Reading Teacher of the Year. Wilson also served in the US Army during Vietnam as a medical corpsman and operating room specialist. Later in life he enlisted in the National Guard and received the Iowa Army Commendation Medal.

Wilson has been an avid Iowa Hawkeye fan since childhood. His first football game was the 1957 Rose Bowl when he was ten years old (photo on left above). In retirement, he is currently volunteering as an ambassador for The University of Iowa Athletics Hall of Fame and Museum, attending and supporting Hawkeye athletic events, and maintaining his Hawk Room of personal memorabilia from his adventures and experiences as a lifetime Hawkeye.

Mark has been married to his wife, Pam, for fifty years and has two grown children, Jason and Alissa, and three granddaughters... all of whom are Hawkeye fans, too!

The Ice Cube Press began publishing in 1991 to focus on how to live with the natural world and to better understand how people can best live together in the communities they share and inhabit. Using the literary arts to explore life and experiences in the heartland of the United States we have been recognized by a number of well-known writers including: Gary Snyder, Gene Logsdon, Wes Jackson, Patricia Hampl, Greg Brown, Jim Harrison, Annie Dillard, Ken Burns, Roz Chast, Jane Hamilton, Daniel Menaker, Kathleen Norris, Janisse Ray, Craig Lesley, Alison Deming, Harriet Lerner, Richard Lynn Stegner, Rhodes, Michael Pollan, David Abram, David Orr, and Barry Lopez. We've published a number of well-known authors including: Mary Swander, Jim Heynen, Mary Pipher, Bill Holm, Connie Mutel, John T. Price, Carol Bly, Marvin Bell, Debra Marquart, Ted Kooser, Stephanie Mills, Bill McKibben, Craig Lesley, Elizabeth McCracken, Derrick Jensen, Dean Bakopoulos, Rick Bass, Linda Hogan, Pam Houston, and Paul Gruchow. Check out Ice Cube Press books on our web site, join our email list, facebook group, or follow us on twitter. Visit booksellers, museum shops, or any place you can find good books and support true honest to goodness independent publishing projects so you can discover why we continue striving to "hear the other side."

Ice Cube Press, LLC (est. 1993)
North Liberty, Iowa, Midwest, USA
steve@icecubepress.com
twitter @icecubepress
www.icecubepress.com

to Fenna Marie and
your brave wonderful life
from where you've come and how it's
all stretched out before you
your legacy is alive and well and burning bright